All for God's Glory
Redeeming Church Scutwork

Louis B. Weeks

THE
ALBAN
INSTITUTE

Herndon, Virginia
www.alban.org

The Alban Institute
2121 Cooperative Way, Suite 100
Herndon, VA 20171-5370

Cover design by Spark Design

Library of Congress Cataloging-in-Publication Data

Weeks, Louis, 1941–
    All for God's glory : redeeming church scutwork / Louis B. Weeks. p. cm.
    Includes bibliographical references (p. 167).
    ISBN 978-1-56699-379-1

    1. Church growth—United States. 2. Protestant churches—United States.
      I. Title. BR526.W44 2008

    254—dc22

                        2008036044

12   11   10   09   08   VP   1   2   3   4   5

TABLE OF CONTENTS

PREFACE

"Sorry I can't go. I'm snowed under. 'Scutwork,' you know."

I had asked Dale for lunch with a mutual friend. But he faced what he called "The beginning of the *real* church year"—early September, not Advent. I understood. The congregation Dale served was gearing up for a mission trip to Central America, in addition to its regular fall programs. Even with a good team in place, administration in late summer takes much energy to overcome the initial inertia at the beginning of the "real" church year. Dale said he had people to call before the session meeting, letters to write to the fall stewardship campaign leaders, and a Sunday School teacher coming to talk with him about her co-teacher's negative style with the children.

I know what "scutwork" means. It's a euphemism from Navy parlance for garbage, and its lexical cousin "scutbucket" is the garbage can.

It's the unwanted part of work—for leaders in congregations usually the organization and administration of programs and services. And it consists in the necessary enduring of and sometimes the moderating of countless meetings, and the myriad phone and e-mail exchanges to get something "on the table" for consideration let alone to get something accomplished. It is the budget keeping and the constant attention to communication. It frequently does not seem "spiritual" in any way whatsoever, though perhaps Saint Benedict would say its repetitious drudgery helps people "grow into Christ."

Carl Dudley, a pastor and professor who has been a longtime student of congregational life, sees the possibilities, too. He tells me that, "Through the lens of congregational studies, every act of administration is permeated with the motives and consequences of ministry." Carl would not make a distinction between administration and ministry. This book elaborates on some best practices in various areas of congregational life on the parts of pastors, professional and support staffs, and lay leaders of congregations. Indeed, in these situations and with these people, the motives and consequences for administration are thoroughly ministerial; they lead directly to pastoral care. "Best practices" is a term borrowed from professions such as law and accounting that aptly describes a way of congregational leadership as well. I visited numbers of congregations and talked with many of the church leaders I know who do a good job of this ministry of doing church administration in such a way as to increase the measure of pastoral care.

Some of these leaders and some of these congregations were ones I knew from having worshiped and worked among them. Some came to my attention thanks to their reputation of being effective and healthy communities. Constraints of time and money kept me from visiting many more. Those I visited are mostly Presbyterian, the portion of the church with which I have identified. I trust congregational leaders from other denominations can make the necessary translations by analogy. I trust fellow Presbyterians will forgive my slide into common Protestant vernacular, as with the use of "clergy" and "lay" to describe leaders of congregations. Properly speaking, we have neither—only officers and members.

One more prefatory word, please. My life as a student of scripture and of the church through the ages leads me to rely heavily on both the Bible and history. I do think the first believers, who shared life together and from whom came the books of the New Testament, had a keen sense of servant leadership and management in the nascent congregations. More important, I believe the Bible, both Old and New Testaments, provides unparalleled warrants for truth, primary authority for our faith and life. I pray we Christians all share a basic commitment to the inspiration of the Bible.

I am grateful for the collaboration of those interviewed, some old friends and some new acquaintances, people whose names and church responsibilities will be recounted here. All generously provided time for good conversations, and all interpreted insightfully the ministry of their congregations. Almost all after seeing the manuscript gave permission for me to use their names. Their gifts of reality and candor make the argument more transparent and useful.

Through this project, I came to know Phill Martin, Simeon May, and many in the National Association of Church Business Administrators. I am grateful that they permitted me to learn from them, especially for permitting my participation for several months in their CBA Yahoo! Group, which daily offers mutual insight and information among several hundred leaders who serve local congregations.

Thanks also to James Lewis, director of the Louisville Institute, and the referees who provided a study grant for the research undergirding this book. The Lilly Endowment, which supports the Louisville Institute and many other research and capacity-building opportunities for pastors and scholars in American religion, deserves praise for its generosity, but even more for its persistence in seeking the revitalization of American Christianity. I am extremely grateful to Craig Dykstra, Christopher Coble, John Wimmer, and others in the religion section. In fact, officers and staff throughout the Endowment deserve acknowledgement and gratitude.

My deep thanks, also, to Union Theological Seminary and Presbyterian School of Christian Education—board members, faculty, and administration for their support of my project. Special appreciation to Janet Shook, Patrick Coats, Janet Puckett, Jane Sutherland, and Mike Cashwell, who did the scutwork on the grant. Mark Valeri, Ken McFayden, Tom Currie, Beverly Zink-Sawyer, Carol Schweitzer, Ronald Byars, and Bill Arnold (who was there and then left to serve a congregation) have given me insight and wisdom, several of them reading sections of the drafts.

Carl Dudley, Barbara Wheeler, Jack Carroll, and others who have studied congregations gave helpful advice, and some read portions of the manuscript drafts. Others who seriously study congregations are named in notes, and I am grateful for their good work, too.

Richard Bass, David Pratt, James Wind, and colleagues in the Alban Institute committed early to its publication and helped fashion the voice of the book. They secured Ulrike Guthrie as editor, a fine colleague and collaborator, although shortcomings naturally are of course my own. For any that impede learning and growing, I apologize. And I pray that ongoing constructive conversations inspired by this book can help many congregations and their leaders grow in effective ministry.

Louis Weeks
Williamsburg, Virginia

CHAPTER 1

"Bear one another's burdens…"
Church Administration and Pastoral Care

P aul advised the believers in Galatia to "live by the Spirit." He spoke of testing one another, restoring one another in a spirit of gentleness. He said, "Bear one another's burdens, and so fulfill the law of Christ" (Gal 6:2 NKJV; see 5:16–6:10). In ecumenical settings, in denominations, and in congregations, we all seek to bear the burdens of others and help restore one another in a spirit of gentleness. Thus the dichotomy between denominational trauma and dysfunctional congregations on the one hand, and the healthy condition of so many congregations and some church bodies on the other is vexing indeed. What does it mean to bear one another's burdens today, in churches?

The Congregational Puzzle

How—at one and the same time—can there be so many healthy mainline congregations flourishing and faithful in mission *and* such lamenting about the dysfunction of mainstream Protestantism? This project grew from my wanting to learn from and teach about these healthy churches that flourish amid the shifting paradigms that throw others into dysfunction and despair. Why is it that some congregations take pride in their work and worship, their nurture and witness, while others struggle? Why is it that some congregations manage to be self-concerned but not self-absorbed, when others are not?

Pundits have found fault with American mainline Protestantism ever since denominations were "invented" in the new United States of America. In fact, Puritans in the colonies already looked down on many "less adequate" second-generation clergy joining their ranks. A "declension" among believers was consistently lamented. As denominations took form in the new nation, colleges and seminaries were organized to nurture strong religious leaders—first pastors and lay leaders, and subsequently missionaries, Christian educators, musicians, evangelists, and others in every major denomination.

In recent decades this lament has focused on the mainline Protestant loss of members, its retreat from the public square, and its recalcitrance in the face of quantum shifts in American demography, modes of appropriating knowledge, and pervasive distrust of national institutions. Pastors, others on church staffs, and lay leaders in congregations and denominations have been viewed as fearful of, poorly equipped to reach, and out of touch with the spiritual hunger of new generations. Such critical broadsides are scathing, well phrased, and telling in many respects.

In truth, it is no wonder that Protestantism, which began by decrying the shortcomings of the Roman Catholic Church and dividing immediately into fractious groups of believers, should in time be subject to severe critique by adherents and nonbelievers alike. We deserve criticism for our arrogance, borne of decades of power as an informal "establishment," which people joined for social and commercial benefit and whose leaders commanded respect and status in the community.

So today, for a host of reasons, things are quite different. Denominations founded in one American century, adapted well for another, now find it difficult if not impossible to reinvent themselves in a quite different one. Stalwart church dioceses, conferences, presbyteries, synods, and associations find themselves with diminished if not disappearing resources for mission. Many congregations seem befuddled, grasping at straws for worship and work at odds with their historic identity, seemingly led by mediocre if not incompetent people, agonizing as they seek to be faithful to and praise God in their communities of work and worship.

At the same time, thousands of congregations and not a few regional church bodies thrive. Despite the imperfections of any institution involving human beings, lay leaders still emerge with confidence and competence to guide ministries and evangelism initiatives. These congregations include small and large churches, with worship in both "traditional" and "contemporary" styles (some in both), doing mission of all sorts, and situated variously in cities, suburbs, and rural areas. Their congregational worship is joyful, nurturing, and attractive to visitors who gladly join the fellowships. Excellent music, appropriate and educated reading of scripture, pertinent preaching, and reverent prayer characterize the services. Educational and outreach efforts are effective. Good stewardship of resources and time is evident.

As Mary asked the angel, "How can this be?" (Luke 1:34)

We ask, How can such healthy, faithful, and joyous witness occur in the midst of such religious confusion and dysfunction? Surely it is by God's grace. As the angel responded, "Nothing will be impossible with God" (Luke 1:37).

The beginning of decline in Presbyterian membership, and the onset of other of our problems, coincided with my ordination as a Presbyterian forty years ago, so I have done my share of lamenting about Protestant problems and Presbyterian predicaments.

But for forty years, it has also been my privilege to work and worship in hundreds of fine congregations, among folk who hear and obey the gospel as the Bible enjoins believers to do. I have wept tears of respect for Sunday school teachers, youth leaders, and Bible teachers in whose lives we can see the scriptures at work by the power of the Holy Spirit. I have been inspired and moved by the fine preaching and prophetic leadership of pastors, educators, musicians, administrators, and others in congregations. Time and time again, I receive the gifts of the Spirit through the thoughtful, imaginative witness of Christians. In my wildest dreams for the church, those receiving gifts of the Spirit share them broadly so all can grow in the love of God and love of neighbor.

The Gifts of the Spirit

The gifts of God's Spirit are many, as Paul reminds us in speaking to Galatians and Corinthians alike—gifts of wise utterance, healing, tongues, interpretation, prophecy, discernment, life, joy, peace, patience, faith, hope, love, and more (1 Cor. 12; Gal. 5). The letters to the

Corinthian Christians attest that healthy communities of faith exist only by God's grace and by leaders with true, spiritual gifts. Paul evidently hoped that believers in Corinth would receive God's spiritual gifts in heaping measure, discern them in one another, and learn together the joy and faithfulness of life in Christ. Those gifts of the Spirit, also termed "weapons of the spirit," permit ordinary believers to accomplish extraordinary things.

So while spiritual gifts are from God, not conjured by our efforts, we also hone the gifts and use them, share the gifts and pray their presence in full measure for one another according to God's providence. I am reminded of the 1989 movie *Weapons of the Spirit,* a documentary by Pierre Sauvage. He returned to Chambon-sur-Lignon, where he had been hidden during World War II and rescued from the Holocaust, as had several thousand other Jewish refugees. Sauvage interviewed members of the French Reformed, or Huguenot, congregation to discern their source for such courageous, sacrificial, and dangerous actions. He learned that numbers of them, especially their pastors, had been teaching and practicing simple discipleship for years. When crisis came, they were not paralyzed. They knew to bear one another's burdens. Their educated instincts led them forward in effective ministry, even at considerable personal sacrifice, potentially martyrdom. They responded to human need—as one said, "Normally, like Jesus taught us to do."[1]

Gifts of the Spirit, "weapons" of the Spirit, regular study of Scripture, small groups meeting for prayer in homes, theological discussion of sensitive issues of politics and morality, organization for aiding the poor, and others were evident in that congregation, joyful and faithful in work and worship. They are sometimes very apparent. And we all delight when we receive the benefits from them.

Some years ago, a county seat congregation in the Blue Grass section of middle Kentucky invited me to preach for a celebratory occasion, a church anniversary. As we geared up together for the worship, I noticed how well prepared they were for me and for visitors more generally, how organized the educational program seemed for such a small community of the faithful. The clerk of session, in leading me thoroughly through the order of worship, also alerted me that one member of the congregation with cerebral palsy would be in attendance, a simple administrative action on her part.

Sure enough, when a Call to Worship came, it was answered vocally by a helmeted young man, restrained in a wheel chair. When we sang, he sang in monotone according to my ears, a dissonant, incomprehensible song. When I began to preach, he did too. At each occasion, I could see the inquisitive faces of the members of the congregation, saying in effect, "You got a problem with that?" The clerk's simple administrative act of noting their particular situation helped me prepare for and indeed enjoy a unique form of call-and-response preaching. Hers was an act of pastoral care, extended to a visiting preacher.

Both the Huguenot community and this rural Kentucky church engaged effectively in congregational administration, as well as in authentic preaching and teaching—preparing people for witness and mature worship. In fact, as Pierre Sauvage shows of the Huguenot community, prophetic witness grew directly from mundane routines within the congregation. In Kentucky, that small Bluegrass congregation was first off the starting block in ministry to Spanish-speaking migrant workers. Presbytery leaders opined that their organization and their regular, inclusive life together prepared them for exceptional outreach. Both congregations of Christians exuded a quiet sense of fulfillment and even joy in their faithfulness.

Preparation, organization, and other administrative duties are crucial for effective programs and mission in a congregation, as elsewhere in society. Preaching, teaching, and pastoral care—the three indispensable parts of congregational life that comprise its core—all depend upon adequate congregational administration. Mission, witness, outreach, and service, which emanate from healthy congregational life, likewise result from good church management and leadership.

Since some other parts of congregational life receive more concerted attention in books and workshops, and since this matter of administration as pastoral care has been comparatively neglected, I explore in this book ways in which churches are engaged and can engage in practices of administration to deepen care for members and others in the society. What do I mean by administration and pastoral care in the congregational context? And what is the difference between management and leadership?

Congregational Administration

Church administration is exceedingly complex. It consists of obvious tasks: making and keeping budgets; planning and assessing programs and activities; organizing worship and work efforts; enlisting officers, teachers, and staff, as well as dismissing those who cannot effectively carry out their responsibilities. But it also consists of subtle and systemic perspectives, for good planning makes for excellent worship and nurture; mission and witness are inextricable from effective organization; deep, trusting partnerships among pastor, staff, and lay leadership are built on keeping promises and meeting responsibilities; and, in the words of the popular 1954 song, sung by Kitty Kallen, "Little Things Mean a Lot." The administration of a church, a congregation, includes myriad little transactions—words and actions that organize, plan, prepare, assess, and oversee the work of the congregation.

Church administration is exercised in every congregation by numbers of people—including the circle leader, the youth advisor, the bookkeeper, the music director, the ushering coordinator, the custodian, the member of the governing body keeping minutes, the deacon setting up a visit—as well as by the pastor and ministry staff. And healthy congregations rejoice in good people accomplishing the tasks well together, but even more in the sense of collaboration and mutual benefit that comes from a concerted perspective concerning congregational care.

The extent, complexity, and breadth of church administration surprises everyone engaged in ministry, whether pastor, member of church staff, or lay leader. So many issues vie for attention and resolution, resolutions increasingly temporary in scope: What is lined out in a budget? Off budget? What software? What furniture? What wedding, funeral, baptism, communion policies? Nongluten wafers? Nondripping candles? Criminal background checks—on volunteers who care for children? All volunteers? What about newsletter typos? Licenses? State employment regulations? Each leader in a congregation can make a "To Do" list that keeps on growing. It is these concerns to which I turn in chapter 2.

We have tended to treat the efforts in administration as discrete *tasks* of management. After chapter 3 on the history of the subject, chapter 4 considers *best practices* in congregations, with careful observations of two congregations that seem to "have it all together." A fabric of mutual expectations for good administration underlies a coherent identity in mission, worship, education, and care. As you read the congregational leaders' stories of their work, and as you follow their engagement in specific meetings, decisions, and relationships, you can gain perspective concerning both their patterns of behavior together and their theology of congregational life. You can also see how the work of administration opens and enhances the pastoral care in those churches.

In my research I found that congregational leaders kept naming obstacles in addressing administrative concerns and tasks. They called them variously "temptations," "seductions," "excuses," and "rationales" that got in the way of effective work and inhibited pastoral care. Chapter 5 addresses some of these so-called temptations. In speaking with church leaders, I found they actively fought against certain inclinations and proclivities. And it seemed worthwhile to name several; doing so often helps prevent us from succumbing to them.

Chapters 6 through 10 continue the exploration of particular congregations that are exemplary in some distinct areas where church administration can be discerned as bearing on pastoral care—governance (6), visiting members (7), stewardship (8), worship (9), and "letting go" in administration (10).

Most of the congregations selected for study in one area also excel in other areas of church life as well. I chose each because I knew leaders there would grant me hospitality and access to their processes for administering the work. Moreover, the congregations had respect from other church leaders in the area, reputations and histories fitting for the project. Most of the congregations and leaders chosen were Presbyterian, for my experience has been largely among that portion of the Christian family.

Finally, from the findings gathered from among these congregations, chapter 11 explores some of the pastoral elements of administration that facilitate pastoral care. In both administration and in pastoral care, leaders in congregations help the whole community to bear one another's burdens.

A Word about Pastoral Care

If there is a professional identity in congregational leadership, there is also a charismatic one—especially for those on the staff. We seldom elevate "shamans" these days, who seek by magic to conjure the otherworldly realities for our benefit. But we do expect that religious leaders will be able to focus spiritual life for the rest of us. That focus is best termed "pastoral care." Today, not only the pastor, but *certainly* the pastor, provides pastoral care, the widest form of ministry. Others among the pastoral and church staffs also give pastoral care, as do lay leaders—even in priestly streams of Christianity, whether Orthodox or Western Catholic.

Pastoral care, historically termed "the cure of souls" or "the care of souls," is the consummate form of ministry. Pastoral care is provided in preaching, teaching, counseling, mutual confession, modeling Christian practices, and a variety of other activities. Chapter 2 explores both the history and nature of congregational pastoral care and examines what is at times perceived as the uneasy relationship of care and administration for church leaders today. For since the rise of psychiatry and psychology, the care or cure of souls has frequently been seen as the domain of professionals who counsel. Congregational leaders, pastors included, are generally warned against undertaking pastoral counseling unless they have undergone clinical apprenticeships in the discipline. As one seminary professor put it emphatically, "Refer as quickly as you can! You can get deep, quickly!" Granted, pastoral counseling is extremely helpful for some people, and prolonged counseling requires expertise. But it does not supplant the more general and usually more necessary pastoral *care*.

Pastoral care is a much broader enterprise than pastoral counseling. If pastoral *counseling* is seeking the mental and spiritual health of people or groups of people, then pastoral *care* is seeking the spiritual growth of people and congregations and empowering their faithfulness in living and proclaiming the gospel. Pastoral care and pastoral counseling are therefore distinct disciplines or practices. The latter occurs by focusing clinically on the psychological and emotional health of people who come into a formal setting for extended counseling. For the provider of counseling, it usually involves set hours and appointments; for the provider of pastoral care, opportunities for care arise at almost any time or place.

According to William Arnold, pastoral care is marked by initiative and faithfulness. "Regular visitation stands as the cardinal expression of a caring process that is distinctly pastoral," he asserts.[7] Sometimes it's a knowing smile or a well-phrased letter. Arnold says, "The highest skill in pastoral care is providing it so effectively that it's natural, not recognizable as such. Ultimately, pastoral care builds the trust zone among Christian believers and opens the faith for others."

The phrase "pastoral care" issues directly from scripture, in the allusions to Jesus as shepherd and disciples as assuming responsibility for the sheep. Pastoral care comes also from Christian theology: it exhibits and embodies God's grace reaching out to us and our subsequently responding. It also involves both belief and action.

Pastoral counseling is also supposed to be pastoral care, as is the more recent subset of counseling, "pastoral psychotherapy." But pastoral care is not exhausted in counseling, and certainly not in psychotherapy. Pastoral care extends to all the ways in which human beings are faithful—being present for others in joy and in sorrow, helping one another grow in Christ, and through ongoing teaching and learning.

Initiative and faithfulness, the two marks of pastoral care Arnold identifies, are both features of the human character. The person with zeal for the gospel and deep love of others will take initiative in relationships with others. And the person seeking to be faithful to God will also practice promise-keeping with neighbors. Healthy congregations feed on both marks of pastoral care, and energetic people faithful in relationships are the bedrock of congregational vitality and joy. Human? Yes, and with foibles, but also regularly dependable, people others can count on.

Yet initiative and faithfulness are not only character traits, so to speak. They are also activities directly related to administration. Enlisting volunteers, assessing staff, planning programs, and hosts of other such organizational efforts exhibit and model initiative. Budget making and keeping, strategic planning, and following through to meet goals and accomplish priorities—crucial matters at the core of administration—are equally matters of faithfulness. Church administration and pastoral care are inextricably connected. In fact, in many best practices in congregations, they really are much the same thing, almost indistinguishable. Writing a letter to provide an inquiring family with church guidelines for weddings is an act of administration. Writing a personal letter to provide information about church guidelines and to invite them into conversation about *Christian* weddings is an act of pastoral care.

Many good congregational leaders, even if they have not explicitly focused on the interrelationships between church administration and pastoral care, engage instinctively in church administration *as* pastoral care. Almost all tell me that they also concentrate constantly upon improvement in both areas, if indeed they have not yet merged the functions in their own minds.

Some who engaged church administration only as a necessary evil without appreciating its interconnections with pastoral care also engage the work effectively today. They have learned how important is good church administration and speak of the change they experienced in satisfaction and joy as they grew aware of and proficient in good administrative practices. Good analogies and metaphors can help bring alive matters of leadership. Think, for example, of the symphony conductor, an image frequently employed in exploring leadership. Or of the elegant group flight of waterfowl.

The Symphony Conductor

Years ago, when we lived in Louisville, we had the privilege of attending some orchestra rehearsals led by George Schram, a friend who served for a time as resident conductor of the orchestra. My friend the conductor listened and read—"prepared" the music—in both his memory and his "body," if you will. Members of the orchestra also prepared, and before rehearsals you could hear them working on particularly difficult musical passages. An orchestra librarian distributed the music before the rehearsal. The sound and light people prepared, too. When everyone assembled, they anticipated together the changes, the transitions, repeating tough musical challenges and, in the words of the conductor, "getting them right." Getting the music right meant in accord both with the music on the page, the talents of the musicians, and the conceptual imagination of the conductor.

Just how important the skill and intuitions of the conductor were became apparent on one occasion when a young man, who had won at auction the privilege of conducting, came to rehearse the piece he would lead. Rehearsals seemed routine, even mundane, until I observed this novice step boldly to the podium and begin wanly to wave his baton and arm. Blatant discord ensued, though professional musicians still made the piece sound acceptable even for a conductor who had no practice (and skills to match!). Frustration showed first in the timpani, which were a half-beat early on one incursion, then in the woodwinds. The strings seemed impervious until one kept going when the rest stopped. When they were through, the trombone played a final "whinny" of disgust. After the young man left in a fancy car, my friend said to the orchestra, "Let's do that again!" They all laughed and began the hard work of rehearsing. The resulting performance made the young dilettante look undeservedly adept at conducting, and it garnered him—rather than George Schram and the orchestra—a standing ovation. The conductor and the orchestra might be seen to have borne the burden of the amateur interloper, but they did it joyfully together.

Gradually, in working with congregational leaders, I came to see that this image of conducting an orchestra applies for many types of leaders, not just for pastors. And the notion of rehearsal—rather than of the administration undergirding a performance—brings together all the skills of all the "players" in leadership. Like the case of the young man who won a chance to conduct the orchestra, I have been amused occasionally to see even the inadequate leader receive the congregational equivalent of a standing ovation on account of the back-channel work of selfless authentic leaders!

The image of the church leader as orchestra conductor sadly lends itself at first to thinking of singular leaders. Yet church administration that enables pastoral care to happen is inherently a team affair. What image could we choose that would reflect more accurately the situation for congregational leaders?

Recently we attended a concert featuring James Galway, the renowned Irish flutist. The "Pied Piper Fantasy," which Galway had commissioned from John Corgliano, asked in one portion for the strings and woodwinds to be engaged in sweeping and romantic music, while the drums and some brass followed quite a tight metric "chorale." Suddenly, without introduction, one of the French horn players stood in place, and he moved his arms stiffly as a human metronome, keeping that strong counter beat. Of course, as he faced the audience, he also faced the conductor, JoAnn Falletta. It looked as though he was contradicting her leadership, but actually he was supplementing it, at her request. Portion completed, he sat down and again assumed his regular function as a horn player. This "second conductor," working at odds with the flowing, graceful movements of conductor Falletta, accomplished alongside her what one conductor simply never could have done alone.

Later, about twenty teenage flutists and two young snare drummers answered the Pied Piper's flute and joined in the music, marching through the auditorium and ultimately going on stage with James Galway. At the close of the piece, as Pied Piper Galway piped the "children" off stage right with his gold flute, he carefully provided conductor Falletta with the penny-whistle flute he had previously employed. She began to play the tune as well, and she marched out stage right at the end of the line of flutists and drummers.

I inquired after the performance and learned that conductor Falletta had determined to employ the "counter conductor," and that Galway had told Falletta in rehearsal that he would be handing her the penny whistle. The seeming creative spontaneity had indeed been creative. But it only seemed to be spontaneous—all the better to entertain!

High-Flying Geese

A radically different image also illumines for me the management and leadership of a congregation for mutual care and growth in witness. Out of our back window most mornings we can see and listen to geese awakening and organizing to fly to the nearby grain field. Geese are extremely messy on the ground, clumsy and irritating. As they prepare to fly, different ones flap wings and call to one another. Are they cajoling? It certainly sounds like it. At any rate, as if on a signal, the majority—if not every one of them—takes to the air simultaneously, and they "form up" quickly into a vee or two as they gain altitude and speed. Their beauty will take away your breath, and their honking to any geese still swimming soon summons the remainder into flight.

A provocative book by Browne Barr, *High-Flying Geese: Unexpected Reflections on the Church and Its Ministry*, explores that novel image for pastors and other leaders of congregations. The marvelous, extended metaphor Barr exploits is that of the flight of gaggles of geese.[3] He plays with the fable of "The Domestic Goose," from the *Journals* of Søren Kierkegaard, for example, with the gradual fattening of a wild goose who keeps preaching flight and freedom among a flock of domestic geese. Finally, it is the wild goose that is tamed, rather than the domestic geese learning freedom in flight and the adventures of migration.

More to the point of effective administration for the cure of souls are the marks of flying geese Barr discerns—saving energy in formation, sharing the lead position, honking from behind, and, "keeping company with the fallen." Barr quotes zoologists who claim that geese in formation fly 70 percent faster than does a lone goose. Even the lead goose gets an aerodynamic boost from the formation. And the goose in that position shares the lead, contrary to popular opinion, thereby improving the flock's range enormously. Geese honk from behind not to complain, apparently, but as encouragement both to those in formation and to others who might join. Finally, Barr tells us that geese will frequently remain with those wounded or lame, urging them toward health and flight.

Each of these marks of flying geese applies to church leadership. Well led, a congregation can serve the healing and nurture of so many more than any one person's individual effort, no matter how heroic. Out of the relationships come inspiration and learning for everyone, leaders included. Shared leadership in administration is so patently healthy it bears little additional comment, but consider how strong the power of self-sacrifice discussed previously can be.

Most leaders are inclined to hear honking from behind as complaints. And yet profound analysts of leadership encourage leaders to value the honking—whether it is encouraging or critical! Sometimes the best insights come from those least likely to receive a hearing. And the inclusive congregation, like that Bluegrass church of which I wrote earlier that keeps company with the "fallen," demonstrates in its work and worship the grace of God, the self-giving of Jesus in his ministry and even to his death on a cross.

Leadership and Management

Whether for geese or for congregations, leadership is crucial. Recently, many books on leadership in general and church leadership in particular have contrasted being a leader (good) with being a manager (bad). Leadership is perceived as making transformations and giving people a vision by which to live, while management is perceived simply as perpetuating the status quo. Interestingly, no such distinction occurs in either the Bible or in pre-twentieth-century literature concerning discipleship or Christian life.

If there is a distinction, and I think there is one, it exists in leadership as marshalling resources for adaptation, and management as making sure resources are in place to accomplish the desired outcomes. That means letters written, budgets met, meetings attended, and people gaining competence and confidence all come from good management and allow for successful leadership.

This fascinating distinction concerning leadership and management can be followed as the explorations of congregational leadership unfold. And several newer incumbents in positions of congregational leadership and management open the conversations.

Living by the Spirit, as Paul promised the Galatians, would reap life eternal. Where in the orchestra one plays or conducts is not so significant as the making of beautiful music. Where in the vee formation of flying wildfowl one is located pales in comparison to other matters—such as increasing the range for feeding and nesting, protecting the flock, and making the incredible migration. Just so, following scripture, mutual forbearance, mutual restoration, and increasing the range and scope of the church's mission are the significant issues, worthy of exploration.

CHAPTER 2

"It is not right..."
The Ministerial Surprise of Scutwork

"It's not what we expected! It's more than we bargained for."

The cry first came not from pastors, members of church staffs, or lay leaders in churches in contemporary North America, but from the very first Christian leaders—the twelve apostles. "It is not right that we should neglect the word of God in order to wait on tables" (Acts 6:2). "Waiting on tables" may have been the first church administrative task. The term applies not just to cooking and placing food before diners but also to financial provision for life. The apostles had called the whole community together to complain.

We may complain in turn that they had not yet heard Jesus, who had told them that the first should be last and that they should serve, not be served. But Acts says the twelve had a constructive plan—to elect seven Spirit-filled, wise leaders to receive the new task of waiting on tables. And the community received the charge with pleasure. They elected seven, including Stephen and Philip, respectively the first martyr (Acts 7:58–60) and the evangelist to a Gentile courtier (Acts 8:26–40).

Surprise comes frequently in scripture—to Sarah, Samuel, Ezekiel, Jonah, Elizabeth, Mary the mother of Jesus, and Paul, just to name a few, and to the faithful today, as Mike Smith reports. Serving as the Church Business Administrator at Highland Presbyterian Church in Louisville, Kentucky, Mike said he was greatly surprised to learn that in his congregation people vastly different in political views and

social location could be such good colleagues. "They love each other!" He stammered to express his amazement.

Administrative surprises arrive in boatloads for those who serve
as pastors, associate pastors, Christian educators, musicians, youth
leaders, and others who support congregational life. Here, we follow
just a few of those recently entering service to hear their particular
stories of the unexpected.

Don Simpson, Pastor

Don Simpson was not new to ministry. First as a dedicated lay leader, then as a lay pastor, he had preached and led congregations for
several years before attending seminary. But he was surprised at the
amount and the complexity of administrative tasks for which clergy are
responsible when he was ordained in 2007 and charged with leading
the Purity Presbyterian Church in South Carolina. Once a church of
750, the congregation had declined to fewer than 300 as the town and
county lost population as a result of the textile mills closing and the
steady urbanization that robbed rural areas of younger and more afflu-
ent families.

The Christian educator, the administrative assistant, and even
the sexton of Purity had left during the interim between pastors,
as the town's broader population also declined. In his first year,
Don and the lay leaders went through five secretary/administra-
tors, each of whom was responsible for fewer and fewer tasks. So,
much of the regular work that staff had done previously fell directly on his desk—copying letters, printing bulletins, even changing light bulbs.

Don explained that little mistakes frequently led to big conversations and complaints. Typos appeared in the hastily printed Sunday
bulletins. "I asked those who complained to come and proof read," he
lamented. "But when they came and proofed, they still missed some
spelling and punctuation, and then yet others would complain."

More important work—seeking Sunday school teachers, notify-
ing women of their circle meetings, training people to be ushers and
serve communion, and such—fell directly on his shoulders. "I know I
should be visiting more," he said. "I wish I had time."

Don Simpson found the Purity Church plagued by personnel is-sues—perhaps the most critical concern for a church leader who is trying to build a team. He found that he could succeed in having good people hired only if the various committees and governing bodies began working together. He said the system seemed inordi-nately complex for such a little church, in part because many con-gregation members remembered when the church and town were much larger communities.

Likewise, Don discovered that soliciting volunteers fell almost en-tirely upon his shoulders—a situation again quite common among congregations. Perhaps his predecessor had simply wanted to con-trol personally all the invitations to serve, to hand-pick officers and teachers for the church. More likely, the members figured they had "hired" someone to do the selection of church leaders amid all the other tasks. But how to move the church toward greater trust among the officers and a willingness to step out in naming qualified leaders and, together with the pastor, eliciting their service?

Along with all of these tasks, of course Don is also expected to preach good sermons, lead worship, visit in the homes of mem-bers, see them in the hospital, and call on prospective members. This matter of visiting in homes and hospitals is a crucial and complex part of pastoral care. Don realizes this and says that vis-iting begins with administration, and there may be as much ad-ministration in timing visits effectively and keeping straight the needs of members as there is pastoral care in the actual visits. Still, "They're great folks and I love them," Simpson declared. But, "If we could organize a team, it would be lots better for everyone. Especially for me."

The Plight of Pastors

For pastors, the call to service and leadership anticipates preaching, teaching, administering the sacraments, helping people in need, and building wholesome and healthy congregations. Frequently those moving into pastorates also envision themselves helping whole com-munities, cities, and societies become more humane, peaceful, and just—as the Bible says we should be. Instead, frequently their plight is that the mere taking care of routine congregational administra-tion saps so much time and energy that they have little left over to do what seems to them the real work of ministry. At the same time, in churches large and small, many pastors can be observed engaged effectively in pastoral care, teaching, and preaching, with everything seeming to fit together nicely.

Don Simpson, a competent and mature Christian, shepherds a congregation of sincere, dedicated Christians, but he struggles to organize so he can provide more pastoral care. He struggles in part because of his surprise at the immense administrative load, in part because he is newly engaged in pastoral ministry, in part because of temporary exigencies at the church such as typing bulletins and changing bulbs, and in part because of factors beyond his control—depopulation, congregational memories of many hands on board, and patterns he inherited from previous pastoral styles. Can Don Simpson maintain personal and congregational equilibrium in this maelstrom of demands? Can he and the thousands in his situation find support from others, build a team for ministry, overcome congregational nostalgia, and shift the culture of Purity Church to meet new circumstances?

Paying the Rent in a Holy Calling

Some years ago, a pioneer in studying congregations focused upon this need for religious leaders to attend carefully to organization and administration as well as to preaching, teaching, and pastoral care. James Glasse, a professor at Vanderbilt and subsequently the president of Lancaster Seminary, said that pastors could be classified as being either builders, owners, or renters.

According to Glasse, a few religious leaders "inherit" their congregations and their authority from their fathers, and in a sense "own" them (like Robert A. Schuller or Joel Olsteen), while some plant their own congregations (Rick Warren or T. D. Jakes). Their relationship to their congregations may be a bit different because the congregation grew directly from their personal aspirations. Most pastors, however, are called to serve and lead for a time in an existent congregation, as Don Simpson has been. These Glasse calls "renters"—those pastors and staff who are only with a particular congregation for a limited time before they retire, finish their terms of service, or move to another responsibility.

In most congregations lay leaders as well are elected and called for a particular term of service. In essence, as stewards in leadership, they also gain authority to make changes by "paying the rent." Glasse explained that for pastors, paying the rent means leading worship services that are "acceptable," teaching and offering pastoral care that stimulates faith and provides caring that is mature and "available," and good administration and organization. "What most parishes want, and have a right to expect, is a stable membership, a balanced budget, a building that is in reasonable repair, and organizational leadership that assists them in the parish mission."[1]

The expression Glasse coined for pastors in the 1960s is applicable to every staff member and lay leader in every congregation. "Paying the rent" became a frequent expression among pastors almost immediately, and it remains a good way to think about the necessary administration and organization in church leadership. Glasse did not speak in superlatives—the fastest-growing membership, the exploding resources, or the best-kept buildings. He spoke of adequacy and dependability in administration.

Early in the exploration of "leadership" in congregations, Glasse indicated that permission and freedom to pursue other opportunities beyond the basics can only be granted to pastors who also are sufficiently capable at management. Indeed, too much has been made of the distinction between leadership and management when one is valued and the other debased, as many recent studies seem to do. Not only is "the devil in the details," as the saying goes, but also potential leadership comes from adequately coping with the details and from adequate planning and assessment—managing transactions and operations.

Yet some, like Robert Bacher and Michael Cooper-White, would say that what a pastor is doing in providing adequate administration and balanced budgets is not only "paying the rent" but also a "profoundly holy calling." According to them, "Activities commonly called administration are part and parcel of most ministries, and one whose work is primarily administrative is no less a faithful servant than those who mostly preach, teach, or counsel. . . . It is time for the church to reclaim the holiness of vocations that involve a major measure of administrative work."[2]

Indeed, both expressions are true: church administration effectively both "pays the rent" and is "a holy calling." How many pastors are able to see the work from this perspective? How many devote as much effort to improving skills in leadership and the ministry of organizing structures and thinking systemically as they do to honing skills in preaching and teaching? What can be done to help in this situation?

These are the concerns with which this project began—appropriately naming as a holy calling the administrative tasks that, to many competent, dedicated pastors, seem to usurp ministry. As research progressed, it became apparent that the challenges of pastors are also the problems of others serving and leading congregations as Christian educators, directors of music, church business administrators, support staff, and lay leaders. Further, the plight of pastors is overcome and joy occurs more frequently in ministry, it seems, when all the leaders of a congregation are together meeting the challenges of effective ministry.

Does that same "ministerial surprise" come to others in congregational leadership in various capacities? Listen to some insightful people charged with different responsibilities in local churches, and hear their desires for collaboration.

Whitney Salter, Associate Pastor

Whitney Salter last year joined a high-functioning, multi-staffed congregation in Salisbury, North Carolina. She is charged especially with youth and family ministry, but she finds herself a part of a team engaged in every aspect of congregational leadership. "One could not ask for a better place to start serving churches," she fairly sings of her enjoyment, "or a better group of lay persons, staff, and pastors to work with. They told me the more we prepare and keep things going smoothly, the more we can do—and I believe them."

Even for Whitney Salter in a kind of ideal spot, the surprise of finding that administration was understood by all to be an integral aspect of every ministry—and thus the smooth-running of the church—made her do a double take. "We have this program, 'Teens With a Mission,' that we all call 'TWAM.' It's special for this congregation, and people in the whole town identify it with us. There is reporting in the Salisbury paper, and there are area-wide money-raising projects for the mission."

Whitney explained that each year thirty or more young people and adults go together to work and learn in Mexican churches. "It's a great time for bonding, growing in faith, talking together about life and God and what makes life worthwhile. Last year when I came I realized keeping track of the considerable amount of money is really my job. Soon I was working with an Excel spreadsheet and getting donations regularly, sometimes daily for two weeks running. I do work with a secretary, but I see that such responsible tracking is up to me, because people need to trust that when they make a gift they will get a receipt and an acknowledgement from the youth."

In the fall, preparing for the next summer, TWAM sponsors a 3K run. Runners come from other communities and are sponsored not only by church people but also businesses. Whitney considers all the opportunities she missed the first time she oversaw the event. "Why not ask both the sponsors and runners to come for the celebrations and perhaps for the programs in which those who experience TWAM tell of their experiences? It's all very inspirational, and it might lead some folk to become more interested in our church." She understands that through modest additional administration in this project she can open the door for more ministry opportunities.

Leading From the Second Chair

When I first picked up the book entitled *Leading From the Second Chair*, I thought Mike Bonem and Roger Patterson were employing the image of the orchestra I explored in chapter 1 that is so crucial to my understanding of congregational leadership. Wrong! They were speaking of associate and assistant pastors, folk who in evangelical churches really do frequently sit in the second chair away from the pulpit in the chancel.[3]

Their wisdom, however, deserves attention in considering the special responsibility of those on pastoral staffs who are not senior pastors. Bonem and Patterson encourage associate pastors to dream and plan mightily in accord with their senior pastor's vision. Interestingly, because Whitney Salter is serving with Jim Dunkin, a particularly gifted pastor, she is provided room to be the point person in programs such as TWAM, where she has oversight. In some respects, being the point person adds more to her administrative load because her role is less closely defined than that of some newly minted, tightly supervised associates. And she still must coordinate her plans with Jim's and the rest of the staff and lay leaders. More opportunity for pastoral care may require more rather than fewer administrative underpinnings.

Shirley Rudd, Christian Educator

"Surprise, you bet!" So says Shirley Rudd her first two years in full-time ministry.

> I had been an elder, a deacon, a youth leader, and done lots more in the church before I went to seminary and became a director of Christian education here in Harrisburg. Still, I was surprised by the extent of the administration necessary and important in this congregation—things I never would have imagined.
>
> You know we have a church van, for taking young people and grown-ups to mission activities and trips. I have responsibility for the insurance, the maintenance, and all that for the church van. And, of course, there's no one to do copying for me, to set up the meetings for my various groups, prepare meeting notices, etc. Things like Christian Education Ministry, Shawl Ministry, Youth Council, and lots more are left to me to organize, publicize, and execute—so many things to make the church work well!"

She has responsibilities for teaching, curriculum selection, recruiting volunteers to teach and to plan, preaching and executing special celebrations throughout the year, as well as initiating innovative programs for this church, plus some work in counseling.

Shirley spoke of the inexorable pull of ministerial scutwork and how greatly it impinges on the rest of what she does. "You know, you have a lot of grandiose ideas when you come into a position. I found that I couldn't just start something new. I had to back up and plan step-by-step ways to get things to come to fruition. It takes lots more time than I thought it would."

Process

This "backing up," in the words of Shirley Rudd, is what congregational studies experts often term "process." Attending to process, whether to follow it or to change it, is a major part of administration. In the teaching by Speed Leas and Carl Dudley, process differs from tasks and structure for congregations. Process is the way things get done, the "way the goals are accomplished."[4]

Shirley knew from past experience that she would need to listen, plan, teach, support, and problem solve in order have any innovation in the culture of the congregation. She knew she would need to navigate both formal and informal processes at the Harrisburg congregation. She would need to get permission and funding for a new class from those in formal authority, the session. But from willing teachers, she would also need to receive informally cooperation and hard work in preparing and conducting the efforts.

Shirley found that unexpected and, in her case, seemingly unique responsibilities demanded her complete attention. Insurance and operation of the church van might seem oddly located in her bailiwick. With time, she may be able to pass the responsibility on to someone else. But she came to see that, for the moment, doing the work well permitted mission trips and educational events important for congregational life. The process that was in place was already serving worthwhile ends.

Billy Ricketts, Church Business Administrator

"This is my second church as administrator," Billy Ricketts smiled. "The first one had almost two thousand congregants, and this one has two hundred. I've been surprised in both situations!" Ricketts explained that in his previous job he had engineered and installed sound systems for large buildings. Increasingly, he worked on church systems more than any other kind of installation. As an elder at Second Presbyterian, Norfolk, Virginia, he began to consider some kind of church vocation. He responded to the invitation from the pastor of Norfolk's First Presbyterian Church, Jim Wood, to become the church business administrator (CBA) for that congregation.

I began taking the courses for certification and working at First, too. I had no idea of the complexity and sheer bulk of issues related to security there, in a downtown church. In that urban location, we worried about teenagers running around in the building and leaving it. We had several folk coming regularly to worship who were mentally and psychologically disturbed, folks who were asking for help or coming just to "hang out." We knew most were fine, but we worried about a couple. As a staff, we had had no background checks and learned we needed them for everyone in sight, it seemed—staff, chaperones for kids, and so forth. We even had to hire a regular security person. An elderly woman ushering was not up to potential physical challenges or confident managing homeless and some threatening people who wandered in, and neither was I equipped that way.

Now on the inside of the church organization, I was also surprised at the quantity and complexity of the church politics that played into decision making. I had been an elder and even clerk of session at Second, but I had no idea of the amount of work involved in seeking nominations and eliciting leaders from the laity, all it takes to move an old building from A/C to heat, and when, and when back. . . . Thank God Jim and the others in leadership had me as a part of the *pastoral staff*, for it meant I could share with others on an equal footing, not just be considered a "bean counter." I even served as worship leader for a Good Friday worship service.

At Second Church, where I work now as director of congregational ministries, I have a wider variety of responsibilities, albeit for a much smaller church. I'm employed twenty-five hours a week, and I have begun annual assessments for all of us and also addressed matters such as computers, whether our software is up to date, whether we use our equipment efficiently, and so forth. All these matters are more complex than I thought. This two-hundred-member church has about the same issues the big one did, just fewer of each kind of issue.

I had to learn more patience, and how to do change gradually. For example, I learned not to change the carpet in the whole church, but to do it a room at a time and listen to responses. And I came see how important it is to get additional, theological education. That's the other part of being accepted as part of the pastoral staff—to be able to engage in pastoral care yourself, to think about it. That's the best part of my certification process—learning administration as ministry—both in the CBA and now in the Certified Lay Pastor program.

Good communication is crucial, too. I keep being surprised when people don't have well-publicized events on their minds or when they don't remember things we have announced. When I arrived at Second Pres., there was a big plasma TV mounted in the Fellowship Hall, for example. I asked how it was used and was told that it wasn't used at all. So I use it for announcements whenever we're in there for fellowship. It gives us another "crack" at getting the word out.

Church Business Administrators

Billy Ricketts holds the title Director of Congregational Ministries, and his responsibilities are particularly broad ones currently at Second Church, extending beyond the regular duties of a church business administrator. But the essence of his work is *ministry* in "church business administration." Though this category of ministerial staff is known to many, it deserves some explanation for others. Frequently, even smaller churches hire people full-time or part-time to superintend visitation programs, canvasses for budgetary purposes, and accounting matters. More than six thousand CBAs belong to the national association, most of those accredited through an extensive educational program, but as with educators and musicians, thousands of others are home grown within congregational life and simply do the best they can.

As with Billy Ricketts, even those specializing in church administration find frustration and surprise in the extent and complexity of the work. Sadly, many church business administrators are not perceived to be part of the pastoral team, though almost all of them will state that they see their job as ministry. In the words of Karen Lee Ackerson, CBA at First Presbyterian Church, Tacoma, Washington, "We have to be part of the ministerial team, or the church misses opportunities for pastoral care." She explains that the pastor sets the tone and provides for staff to work well together. "You have to have a heart for it," she says.

A Common Plight

Each member of the staff possesses a discrete vision of what their ministry comprises. Christian educators envision themselves teaching the faith and growing other teachers who can share the gospel and help all grow in love of God and others. Church administrators take on significant responsibilities—making certain the inner workings of a church staff meet needs of people in the church and more broadly. Music directors equally express their vocation in terms of ministry: "If I'd wanted to perform, I surely wouldn't be playing an upright piano and taking all volunteers," one told me pointedly. "I see the work as ministry." Church officers, too, are willing to serve because they sense a call from God to give back in faith and love some of the gifts they have received.

All these Christians undertake ministry because they care about the Christian faith and the upbuilding of the body of Christ, the church. And all of them are tempted to see administrative work as burdensome, unrewarding, and detracting from the core ministry to which they are called.

The work of administration—arranging for church committees, preparing and managing budgets, attending and perhaps moderating meetings, enlisting staff and volunteers, overseeing church policies, engaging in strategic planning, selecting liturgy and music, even answering the mail and e-mail—all consumes time and energy. As communication possibilities increase, so too do organizational problems. And as our loyalty to organizations diminishes, it becomes more and more tempting to treat the church as an organization and less and less as a deep personal and communal response to God's saving work in Jesus Christ. Some would say that spirituality, as distinguished from religious expressions of praise and thanksgiving, does not require organization or even participation with others in worship. In fact, some would say that they are most spiritual when not bothered by others at all. No community, no problem!

In such a demanding spiritual and religious climate, expectations on religious leaders are multiplied. These demands are expressed in terms of requirements. Moreover, these demands are immediate in many cases, seeming to sap time and energy from leading worship and teaching, and especially from the preparation for these functions. They even seem frequently to interfere directly with pastoral care—seeing people in sickness and grief, or just being with those in the congregation on a regular basis for establishing relationships and conversing about faith and life.

If pastors and staff folk are surprised that so much time is necessary for administration, the volunteer lay leaders are often even more astounded. Leaders in most congregations can name individuals who simply resigned from office because they could not afford to spend the time required to oversee and administer committees or projects. One pastor reported that a lay leader chosen for the governing board told him after two meetings: "I can't take this any more. I'll double my pledge if you let me resign from the board."

Research on the Subject

This perceived unexpected burden of time spent on administration is borne out by the research of sociologist Jackson Carroll. Examining the work of clergy, he found Catholic priests, mainline Protestant pastors, "conservative Protestant" (sometimes called "Evangelical Protestant") pastors, and pastors in predominantly black churches all spent significant amounts of time administering the work of the congregation.[5] Of these, Catholic priests spent the largest percentage of their time on administration, while pastors of black churches spent the least. According to one of the studies comprising the report, time spent by mainline Protestant pastors on general administration and leading congregational meetings had actually declined (from a 1954 estimate) when a 2001 survey indicated about 10.5 hours a week generally spent for these tasks. The self-rating scales, however, also showed a more significant decline in the workweek as a whole, down from 66.7 hours a week in 1954 to only 50.8 in 2001. In every case, a significant portion of the week was spent in administration—more than in pastoral care, whether that was understood as counseling, visiting the sick, or other tasks.

More striking, Carroll found that pastors feel less well equipped to deal with administration than with any other pastoral function (except that of converting people of other religions.) Interestingly, among the various pastoral functions, administration was assigned low priority by Protestant lay leaders of all stripes.[6]

Jackson Carroll, James Glasse, Robert Bacher, and Michael Cooper-White are not the only ones providing research and assistance in this direction. Since at least the 1960s, following the pioneering research by Sam Blizzard, groups of sociologists and other analysts of American religion have asserted that every single person with church responsibility is surprised by the amount of time they end up spending on administration. Early research and publications by James Hopewell, Carl Dudley, Barbara Wheeler, and Loren Mead—a "Gang of Five" with Carroll and funded by a grant from the Lilly Endowment—explored the issues for many others. From the beginning, this group of researchers eschewed any "recipe for salvation." Barbara Wheeler remembers that they wanted to provide accessible ways for congregations and judicatories to learn about and respect the individual cultures and identities of Christian congregations. William McKinney, Robert Evans, Nancy Ammerman, Stephen Warner, and others who soon joined in these groups have also shed light on the nature of congregations and the roles of leaders in them. More recently, editors of and contributors to *Church Leadership* have given sage advice and counsel on how to meet and surmount the challenges of church administration. A number of works by members of the congregation studies group will provide insights throughout this book.

It was Loren Mead, one of the Gang of Five, who along with Speed Leas, Ed White, and others who served as consultants with congregations and pastors began to write helpful studies. They engaged in research efforts together that eventuated in the founding of the Alban Institute in 1974. More recently, under the leadership of James Wind, Alban Institute work has focused on a wider array of church matters, offering continuing education and lifelong learning events as well as congregational consulting and resources for congregational leaders..

Beyond organizations such as the Alban Institute, many scholars and teachers have focused on leadership in nonprofit institutions more broadly, and though the church is the body of Christ, it also most certainly is understood in American life as a nonprofit "business." Among the topics discussed are the skills and time it takes to organize and follow through on programs and ministries, congregational cultures and politics, and the transmission of the Christian faith to succeeding generations.

Concluding a recent study of pastors successfully engaged in leading "public churches"—meaning congregations that serve creatively the needs of the poor and marginal—Mark Constantine offers sage advice for all in leadership: "Paying careful attention to the mundane tasks of their work is the one way that pastors earn the trust of their congregations."[7] An inference of this is that ordinary responsibilities well executed, with obvious care for members of the church, yield the trust necessary for pastoral care to be effective.

It helps to see some ways the church has sought through the ages to provide for the care or cure of souls. In every case, administrative work permits deep and effective pastoral care. It is to this I turn in the next chapter.

CHAPTER 3

"Take the purse…"
Has There Always Been Scutwork?

According to Luke, Jesus on his way to Jerusalem first gave the seventy followers instructions not to carry purse, bag, or sandals (10:1–12). Facing his crucifixion, however, he prepared them for the longer service. At Passover table, after instructions that we use as Words of Institution for the Lord's Supper, Jesus told the disciples now "the one who has a purse must take it, and likewise a bag" (Luke 22:30). "Purse," of course, was the word for finances, and "bag" was the word for wardrobe. In other words, those proclaiming needed the wherewithal to travel and settle elsewhere.

Have followers of Jesus always had scutwork? Yes. Every generation of pastors and other church leaders has probably chafed at a part of their duty, or at least enjoyed some responsibilities more than others, and I would guess that scutwork or administration has often headed that list.

In the beginning of the Christian church, disciples, apostles, and other leaders in the new movement occupied offices of religious leadership familiar in both Jewish and Roman religions. Popular Hellenistic mystery religions influenced nascent Christianity as well. Jesus was repeatedly called "Rabbi" ("religious master"), and he was certainly involved primarily in the cure (or care) of souls. "What must I do to inherit eternal life?" was the question posed to him repeatedly, and he responded with questions, parables, new teachings, and collected wisdom from his own Jewish heritage.

Jesus, the religious master, naturally gave direction for pastoral care and for assisting people in gaining wisdom, achieving ethical maturity, and organizing life together. An example of this is one brother sinning against another (Matt. 18). The idea of doing administration as pastoral care pales in comparison to Jesus's sacrifice and commitment to the healing and salvation of people. But readers of the four Gospels may even perceive some pique in Jesus's own ministry when crowds kept coming, when people needed food, and when his healing powers were demanded in the midst of his fatigue (Matt. 9; 16; Mark 6; Luke 17; John 12; and more).

Yet crowd control, holding a "purse" for expenses in common, feeding people, and arranging travel are a few indications that there were menial tasks even in the informal, scarcely organized life of Jesus and followers. And obviously all of the arranging and management was in support of—for the sake of—Jesus's proclamation of the gospel and ministry among people.

The Earliest Followers/Leaders

It is not until Pentecost (Acts 2) and the Council at Jerusalem (Acts 15) that we have scriptural accounts of the ways in which believers in Jesus regulated their life together. The earliest churches, as Jesus's followers organized in various communities, seemed to have had offices—elders, apostles, prophets, teachers, administrators, speakers in tongues, interpreters, and so forth—with only Jesus Christ himself being termed a "priest" in the New Testament writings (Heb. 5). Students of the first centuries of church life are currently pointing to the wide range of Christian organizations and to the import of lay leadership of various kinds in those formal and informal communities of believers. Feeding the poor, leading worship, mission efforts, a major collection across the church for believers in Jerusalem, and securing worship spaces were some of the organizational and management activities named or alluded to in New Testament letters. In these first decades of Christian formation, "elder" (*presbyteros*) was the most common word for a leader in a congregation, and "deacon"(*diakonos*) was a second common title, for those who carried these responsibilities on behalf of fellow believers.

Again we find in these early accounts that pastoral care of believers and of those first hearing the gospel is a central purpose of any administrative work; mission activity is typically the other. Mention of administrative actions and activities is made in the context of telling about the worship, the healings, the preaching, and the missionary travels. The letters from Paul and others are rife with organizational instructions for the new churches. Woe to the believer who acted in a self-aggrandizing manner, or who lied in a matter of stewardship or giving! The Acts of the Apostles tells of the rebuke by Peter and John of Simon the magician (chapter 8), and it recounts the deaths of Ananias and Sapphira (chapter 5), who said they were giving to the common cause more than they actually gave.

Management and Character

By the time of the pastoral letters we receive as 1 Timothy and Titus, leaders had very specific ideas about both the characteristics and the work of church leaders, and this certainly included administration. Notice that the list in 1 Timothy enumerates necessary qualifications for these positions: "Now a bishop [*episcopon*] must be above reproach, married only once, temperate, sensible, respectful, hospitable, an apt teacher, not a drunkard, not violent but gentle, not quarrelsome, and not a lover of money. He must manage his own household well, keeping his children submissive and respectful in every way—for if someone does not know how to manage his own household, how can he take care of God's church?" (1 Tim. 3:2–5)

Furthermore (vv. 6–16), bishops should not be recent converts, lest they fall to temptation. They must have good reputations, not prone to succumb to temptation. Deacons need similar attributes as bishops and also need to be good managers of their households. All must be "tested," the scripture says. Though it uses masculine nouns for the officers, 1 Timothy says women should have the same faithfulness as men in all things. Interestingly, in the New Testament that word "manage" (*teknon*) is only used in reference to church officers—bishops and deacons, and perhaps the women officers as well. Was management ability a perspective or a practice? It seems to have been both.

The brief letter to Titus does not mention management, but it uses much the same language otherwise to speak of bishops and elders interchangeably, people who "should be appointed in every town." In addition to the standards named in 1 Timothy, it requires that a bishop be blameless and have sound theology (Titus 1:5–9).

So we see that already in the earliest church, church administration was directly linked to the pastoral care of believers. Ability to manage and lead was explicitly expected among pastors as the first churches appeared in cities, towns, and in the countryside around the Mediterranean.

Into Establishment

As the new faith spread and endured to another generation and beyond, churches organized more carefully, and church leaders took on many of the characteristics common to other, well-known religions. Priests, as well as elders, deacons, and bishops, are frequently mentioned in the second century and during the subsequent time of the church fathers. Established Judaism had previously supported priesthood, before destruction of the temple during Roman occupation. All the competing religions of that time seem to have had priests as well, so it seems natural that nascent Christianity came to develop such an office. Other offices developed as the Christian church was recognized as an official religion and in many locations became part of the host culture, but church leaders and not just members also increasingly took responsibility for care of the poor and provision of some educational services for whole populations.[1]

In the medieval Christian church, priests, bishops, archbishops, and popes became increasingly powerful, and militant church leadership provoked crusades and purges in efforts to maintain Christian purity and promulgate the gospel. All the while, new religious orders of men and women arose periodically to provide reform and turn attention to caring for the uneducated and the needy. Pastoral care became increasingly tied to the penitential system, and confession of sin together with penance remained a strong and important portion of care—one sometimes trivialized in what Luther later interpreted as simony.

In some respects these extremely well-organized and usually semi-autonomous religious orders offset the increasingly hierarchical central authority. A parish system prevailed in most of the Western church, where geographical areas were served by and supported individual churches and chapels. Dioceses oversaw congregations, and cathedral churches provided religious centers for worship and work in a particular city or region. The marked variety and local diversity in both church organization and the administration of religious orders over time defy simple generalizations such as these. But it is even more problematic to ignore the fact that church administration existed for pastoral care through the established church of the emperors and clerics, monks and nuns of every century. The Protestant temptation to leap from Nicaea to the Reformation does a disservice to this deep truth. In fact, much of the administration of sacraments, forms of worship, perspectives on ethics, and spiritual disciplines still come from these medieval strains of Christianity—both the religious orders and the so-called secular system of priesthood and governance.

Obviously, all of this organization for worship and work required careful planning and programs, capital efforts and various kinds of "taxation." The mutual responsibility exercised between state and church meant that church power was sometimes coercive and membership was usually mandatory. Moreover, Christian vocation was reserved chiefly for priesthood or membership in a religious order. Vocation did apply, however, to political office in some settings, for divine appointment was claimed by earthly rulers as well.

Reformation Vocation and Administration

In every part of the Protestant Reformation and even in the Catholic Reformation of the sixteenth century, new offices and shared power to some degree characterized the movements. Protestants emphasized the "priesthood of believers"—that all baptized received common Christian vocation from baptism and that God's gifts of talents and money should be devoted by everyone to Christian worship and work. In the words of Martin Luther, "See, as no one is without some commission and calling, so no one is without some kind of work."[2] For Luther, vocation was less about self-fulfillment and more about self sacrifice, care for one's neighbor, and care for the whole earth.

John Calvin added a thorough emphasis on vocation as the response of each person in gratitude to God's unremitting grace. So individuals called to be church officers received particular gifts from

God and were consequently responsible administratively for the work of the church. Calvin helped write into the Church Ordinances in Geneva what was expected of church officers. Listen to his words about deacons: "There were always two kinds in the ancient church, the one deputized to receive, dispense and hold goods for the poor, not only daily alms, but also possessions, rents, and pensions; the other to tend and care for the sick and administer allowances to the poor."[3] Calvin also instructed the pastors to work in tandem with the deacons in order to make sure that necessary sustenance was provided for the poor and the sick. In the opinions of both Catholic and Protestant scholars who studied Geneva churches, Calvin's instructions worked, for "Genevan charity was well-organized."[4]

For both Calvin and Luther, responsibility for proclamation of the gospel and nurture of others fell to each and every believer, especially to those gifted for any kind of Christian leadership.

This sharing of the responsibility for church organization and for pastoral care for congregants and nonbelievers alike led in more radical elements of the Reformation—among Mennonites and Amish, for example—to abolishing all ordained offices. Furthermore, the emphasis on God's gifts being given to each believer has continued as a major doctrine for the interpretation of scripture and the discernment of God's will and the Spirit's work. Consider, for example, the Methodist movement, which is centered on reciprocal pastoral care, lay leadership, a system of inclusion encompassing believers, and shared devotion to mission. The genius of organizational "connection" tied every society, class, circuit, and conference tightly together. It offered lay men, and especially lay women, the opportunity to employ God-given skills for the administrative care of fellow believers and for the proclamation of the gospel.

Remembering this long history is frequently helpful and always consoling in the midst of administrative work. The nature of the administrative work varied in different eras, and its center in pastoral care of people was sometimes seen as more indirect and secondary in importance. So as colonial Christians organized American congregations and denominations, they brought with them these perspectives about pastoral care and church life. Reformed Christians, who predominated in most of the colonies, also brought the expectation that a mix of lay and clerical leadership was both biblical and necessary in their own day. This along with a couple of illustrations of organizational work from other times informs our situation today.

Case: Administration of Communion

Take, for example, the periodic pre-communion examination of believers among many Reformed churches during the seventeenth, eighteenth, and nineteenth centuries in North America. The practice seems to have come particularly from the Scottish church, although some other Reformed traditions employed similar examinations following the scriptural admonitions of 1 Corinthians 11. Usually four times a year, elders from the congregation would visit each parishioner's home and inquire about the moral behavior of each member of the family, saying something like, "Have you committed any gross sins this quarter?" Then they would inquire about study of the catechisms, and ask questions and listen for evidence of study. Those responding satisfactorily in both areas of testing received approval, and in some cases communion "tokens" to be presented at the celebration of the Lord's Supper.

After regular worship on Sunday morning, when it came time for the Lord's Supper, pastors and session members would admit to the table those whose examination had been successful. Frequently, in this "fencing the table," they would even read Paul's warning in 1 Corinthians that if people take the meal "in an unworthy manner," they summon God's judgment (1 Cor. 11:27). In addition, they would preach a separate "Action Sermon" for those taking communion, indicating the power of the Holy Spirit in the sacrament to effect change in believers. At this service of communion, leaders would also receive an offering for the poor.[5]

Noteworthy is that the lay leaders of the church in concert with the pastor directed the discipline of members and offered pastoral guidance and rebuke. This was a complex and time-consuming practice, probably not much fun for those testing (and doubtless work as well for each family examined). It did result, however, in high expectations on the part of believers, and it served to reinforce communal family practices of Bible reading, prayer, and study.

The strength of the tradition can be seen in the inspiration for revivals on the American frontier in the early nineteenth century. Settler families on the frontier had gone for months, sometimes years, without communion. Elders could not test the believers' morality and study habits, and pastors were not available to serve communion anyhow. When pastors finally came and offered the Lord's Supper, thousands gathered. But they depended exclusively on the "Action Sermon," preached to the faithful and the scarcely converted alike as the entire preparation for communion. People were by all accounts overcome in this highly charged atmosphere. Their expectations of communion and release from the power of sin resulted in the religious "exercises" that so many interpreted as the work of the Holy Spirit. The Second Great Awakening grew from religious anticipation and the experience of these "sacramental occasions."

Case: Administration of the Sunday School

Another quite different example comes from the development of the Sunday school in most Protestant communions in the nineteenth century. Although some classes were gathered in churches for study during the eighteenth century, mostly on Sunday afternoons under pastoral tutelage, and although organized Christian schools existed throughout most of the history of the church, rigorous organization for evangelism in the early 1800s yielded schools on Sunday morning or evening for the children of the poor. Typically, lay leaders in the congregations, both men and women, administered an extensive educational program on Sunday mornings at the location of the church itself, then in the afternoon at some location accessible for "workingmen," especially the children of struggling or newly migrating white families or the children of African American or Spanish-speaking families. Soon black and Hispanic congregations had their own Sunday schools as well.

Later in the nineteenth century, as extensive networks of Sunday schools developed associations to provide curriculum and instruction for teachers, conference centers evolved and grew both denominationally and ecumenically. Graded curricula were made available in age-appropriate lessons, and schools were developed for educating a coterie of directors of religious education, also termed Christian educators. In most traditions, Sunday schools typically began their gatherings by meeting in "Opening Assembly," where they sang more child-friendly but sometimes militant, triumphal songs than the staid hymnody of congregational worship. Then they divided into graded classes separated by gender. So the fifth-grade boys met separately from the sixth-grade girls in larger congregations, for example, and men's Bible classes met separately from women's Bible classes.

The effects of the Sunday school movement have been mitigated somewhat. The raucous, lay-led, sometimes anti-clerical Sunday schools gave way in most portions of Protestantism to more "domesticated" church school classes led by pastors and professional DCEs, a model that still dominates the imagination for Christian nurture in many congregations and wider judicatories. But both incarnations of this massive effort require effective church administration, with designations of formal "superintendents," solicitation of teachers, selection of curricula, monitoring of classes, sometimes oversight of special music requirements from particular classes ("We need a pianist for the Issues Class, today!"), and so forth.

The Corporate Model for Church Life

In the middle 1980s, when a pastor in eastern Kentucky showed our seminary class around the county seat church he served, he said with feeling, "Now this used to be the pastor's study a hundred years ago!" He pointed to the shelf-lined room in which an IBM Selectric typewriter and some copying machines were surrounded by supplies and a few manuals for operation of the machines. He then took us to an office complex and said with some sense of irony, "See what the ministry has come to!" A suite of offices stood in front of us—outer office with a receptionist, middle office with a secretary, and inner sanctum with his desk, books helter-skelter, and diplomas and mementos on the wall from schools he had attended and mission trips he had led. He lamented that so much of his time was consumed in administration accomplished in this complex of offices that he had little time and no place for study.

As late as 1900, few Protestant churches in the United States had more than three hundred congregants or paid more than a single pastor (modestly). Sunday school leaders, janitors, and choir directors were for the most part volunteers. Dinners were potluck, and stewardship efforts were led for various mission projects by those vitally involved. Mainline Protestant churches had generally ceased to rent pews by that time, replaced by weekly collections during worship. They had also begun to employ capital fund drives in both local churches and denominations.

The nature of administration changed radically as churches grew more complex and "organized," mostly during the early twentieth century. The same kinds of administrative "complexification" show evidence of real staying power as we embark on the twenty-first century. In the early 1900s, as America grew to embrace complex organization as not just necessary but as desirable for businesses and government, denominations and congregations alike changed drastically. Churches—even ones modest in size—began to hire janitors, staff members for Christian education, directors of music for volunteer choirs, workers for congregational mission, and individuals for other responsibilities. Whole new professions evolved—specialists in education, choir directors, mission coordinators, pastoral counselors, efficiency consultants, administrators, and a host of other "experts."[6]

Staff members were called, hired, or both, to do special work that previously had been the purview of lay congregational leaders and officers. Some churches, particularly ones in large cities, expanded quickly to become multi-functional community centers and resources for congregants and the broader public. Urban and suburban churches hired voices to lead the volunteer choirs that "performed," and therefore increasingly demanded anthems, recitals, and pageants. Congregational gatherings for meals, especially in city churches, no longer depended on potluck but rather on kitchens and food preparation, on sets of dishes and people to administer the meals as well as cook them.

Stewardship "experts" invented the double envelope, with perforation between pockets for contributions to pay operating expenses and benevolences, for example, for weekly collection. And liturgical settings were instituted to make the weekly offering a high point in congregational worship. Ushers would bring the collection forward in most churches, and all would rise for a dedication hymn and a prayer. Churches debated whether the collection should come before or after the scripture and sermon, no longer *whether* weekly offerings should be the mode of giving. In some congregations, people were encouraged to split their offering in half, with one half spent in "unified giving" for denominational and mission priorities decided in church bodies, the other in and through the local congregation.

Masters degrees in Christian education (or religious education) began to be offered in the 1910s. Degrees in church music became fashionable about the same time. Certification in "Church Business Administration" began in 1958, and various associations began to certify pastoral counsclors about that same time.

Many more churches remained quite modest in size and resources. Frequently, however, the members and leaders of small churches tried to copy the design and structure of the more complex churches. So the little churches frequently sported nonfunctioning committees and tiny age- or gender-segregated Sunday school classes.

The Role of Pastors

These far-reaching changes also extended to the pastoral role itself. In her Pulitzer Prize-winning biography, Debby Applegate tells of young Henry Ward Beecher, fresh from seminary, serving a congregation in Lawrenceburgh, Indiana, in 1837. "Henry did everything himself: sweeping, dusting, and cutting firewood on Saturdays, opening the church, building the fire, and closing up on Sundays." He raised money to place oil lamps in the sanctuary, which he then had to fill and light each week. Applegate quotes Henry Beecher, "I did all but come to hear myself preach—that they had to do."[7]

The roles of pastors changed drastically, as "professions" and "specialties" captured the imaginations of American Christians in all areas of life. In this way of thinking, one gained increasing competence in one special arena of commerce or profession. No longer just a lawyer, one became a corporate lawyer, a criminal lawyer, or a real estate lawyer. One no longer practiced medicine to meet the whole range of human needs, but rather a physician became a radiologist, a dermatologist, or a surgeon. Even general practice became a medical specialty—frequently termed "family medicine."

In the corporate arena, professionalism led the public and the professionals to discern bankers from mortgage bankers, experts in finance from those in personnel, or sales, or research and development. Competencies also developed, and social locations came to include people with administrative oversight of the corporations as a special kind of business entity—one with "stakeholders" through stock ownership or partnership investments, with boards of directors to oversee policy and exercise prudence on behalf of owners, and with chief executive officers, chief operating officers, chief financial officers, and the like. Laws previously enacted for eleemosynary corporations such as orphanages came to be applied and modified to support both "for-profits" and "nonprofits," a category of entity that included religious institutions and especially congregations.

In such an environment, congregational members and leaders naturally tended to think of church governing boards as prudential policy-makers acting on behalf of "stakeholders"—the members of the congregations—for the most part regardless of traditional denominational policies and structures. Likewise, pastors came to differentiate more clearly the functions in ministry and to specialize as best they could in developing proficiencies in preaching, teaching, pastoral care, evangelism, and even administration. But a congregation needed all the work done in an atmosphere of increasingly professional oversight. Both mature professionals in ministry and lay leaders who read their Bibles knew the church was not a business, but almost everyone in American society lived in world of professionalism. Who would want a pastor deficient in administration or evangelism, let alone preaching, teaching, or pastoral care? According to Brooks Holifield, this new "professionalism" and its corollary, the expectation of administrative oversight of church operations as a requisite proficiency for pastors, occurred suddenly and most pervasively in urban churches. He quotes G. B. Willcox as saying that "there was no call" previously for such skills. Now, "the modern urban pastor needed to find 'a new skill, namely, a work for everyone' and steadily hold everyone to it." Further, Holifield says this administrative expectation for urban pastors meant they were subject to the marks of businessmen—detailed reports, efficiency in operations, deal-making, and, in the words of Albion Small, "the operator of a vast social dynamo."[8]

A critique began immediately of the easy slide into naïve assumptions that congregations and judicatories were "businesses" and that efficiency was the plumb line for measuring success. But, as Holifield points out, Bruce Barton's *The Man Nobody Knows* (1925) showed that Jesus was the consummate businessman, and the "'minister as executive' now permeated the pastoral literature which praised clergy who had 'a splendid executive facility of keeping an organization functioning.'"[9]

By the 1950s, H. Richard Niebuhr, a premier theologian of American Protestantism, could say with certainty that ministers of congregations had become "Pastoral Directors."[10] The awkward term he put forward never gained traction in common usage, but the expectations were certainly there. Both pastors and parishioners embraced them even as they recognized that no one except Jesus Christ could be an expert in either the Christian faith or the proper ways to worship and work together in that faith.

As the churches became more complex, adding educational programs, performance-oriented music, "organized" groups for men and women, girls and boys, neighbors and needy, the pastor was naturally looked upon to superintend at least the overall fabric of these efforts if not the details of administration. And pastoral care itself became for many pastors and congregations confused with and subsumed in a specialty—pastoral counseling.

Pastoral counseling was a specialty that practitioners and advocates quickly codified by building certification processes to gain acceptance and sometimes access to insurance and health care funding. These involved careful diagnosis and extended, formal "work" individually or in groups, to achieve spiritual or mental health for sick, troubled, and dysfunctional people. Pastoral counseling grew as a profession, with clinical practitioners, professional associations, and degree programs in theological education. Many pastors came to focus on pastoral counseling, and some actually turned it into a business, charging for visits and advertising for "clients."[11]

But it was not only in pastoral counseling that the church began to act more like a business; frequently, church leaders also charged fees for celebrating weddings and conducting funerals, and for other janitorial and pastoral services, mostly through the actions of church governing boards. Ordained pastors have served as agents of the state as well, officiating at marriages in most American communions.

Yet this brief history also demonstrates that church administration had existed since the founding of Christian congregations, rather than springing up suddenly and pervasively in urban churches as they became more complex, as Holifield contends. What was different was that the new tools for management and leadership now explicit in other areas of society came to be employed in many congregations, whether urban or rural, and expected in almost all.

The Roles of Staff

The roles of staff likewise underwent a metamorphosis, deeply related to that of pastors' roles but in some ways distinct from them. Assistant pastors, associate pastors, certified Christian educators, certified business administrators, certified directors of children's choirs and handbell choirs, certified dieticians, and many other formal staff positions were developed and regularized in denominational books of operation. Even nondenominational congregations adopted the culture of expectations for staff in similar fashion, though sometimes without the imprimatur from outside bodies for certification.

As staffs developed, the role of the pastor (frequently termed "Senior Pastor," "Head of Staff," or "Head Pastor") assumed more of the supervisory functions—as had likewise happened with authority positions in commercial businesses and other nonprofits. Church leaders frequently decried (and today decry) that churches are not businesses, but they certainly often hold analogous places in Western societies to those of commercial and nonprofit organizations.

Pay and benefits for pastors increased in most churches faster than that of other staff. As with the chief executive officer in a business or nonprofit, care was taken to assure pastors received ongoing education and time for study. Until relatively recently, scant formal education and almost no provision for continuing education designed for ministerial staff members were offered. Staff members learned in apprenticeships of various sorts, and instinctively wise pastors managed nicely to empower and work with members of staffs, both other ministers and paid employees with varying responsibilities. But many more seemed to retain the patterns of simple church leadership, and they delegated responsibility without authority in many cases. Early studies of multi-staffed churches reported that a vast majority of senior pastors considered staff relations to be going swimmingly, while vast majorities of pastoral staff in those same churches reported dysfunction and malaise.

Following pioneering work by Samuel Blizzard in the 1960s, "congregational studies" became a part of practical theology for some theological seminaries. With the consulting work of Lyle Schaller's Yokefellow Institute, and especially with the Alban Institute team led by Loren Mead, attention to and education for pastoral staffs began to flourish in the 1970s. In subsequent decades, general knowledge about the importance of staff relationships has increased, though surprisingly many people still resist formal training and resist spending time together to consider ways they might improve ministry in the congregation together.

At the same time, theological exploration of the necessary church administration within congregational life was taking place. In the late 1970s, Thomas Campbell and others led a movement mostly in seminaries, but sometimes also including pastors and church staffs, to build upon the work of Richard Niebuhr concerning the "Pastoral Director." Campbell argued that "the gift of administration" would be a unifying symbol for congregational leadership, and the pastor could most aptly be termed "minister-administrator." As with the original Puritan label "parson," Campbell suggested that the person of the minister embodied administration—the deploying of the gifts of God among the people of God effectively and faithfully.[12]

On this matter, Campbell began to explore the terms in the Bible and their use in the early church and sought to have seminary curricula integrating disciplines for the education of "parsons-to-be." His part of the new paradigm, represented elsewhere in the Alban Institute, Yokefellow Institute, and Congregational Studies Team, ceased prematurely with Campbell's sickness and death in 1980.

The Roles of Lay Leaders

Pastoral staff and lay leadership roles differ among the various Protestant denominations and congregations. Presbyterians and other Reformed bodies, for example, have lay leaders ordained in similar fashion to the way pastors are ordained. Catholic lay leadership is defined in a complicated manner as well. But the term "lay leaders" can be understood across denominational and confessional bounds. Everyone knows who "lay leaders" are in congregations, whether their authority is formal, informal, or both.

Protestants considered every constructive vocation to be God's call for a person, a location for God's grace to provide fulfillment, avenues for praising God, and faithful service to one's neighbor. Lay offices in Christian churches were considered by most Protestants to be equal in "status" to clerical ones. In fact, among many Reformed portions of Protestantism, believers were simply termed "officers" and "members"—without even resorting to use of the terms "clerical" and "lay." Those in the Radical Reformation movement went even further, deprecating the work of "priests" and "clerics" while asserting the "level ground at the foot of the cross" for believers.

Interestingly, the Anglican portion of the Reformation, which still ordained priests, bishops, and archbishops, found it necessary to accommodate in the American colonies the vesting of lay leaders with considerable authority for local congregational life. So the "vestry" was invented in the American colonies as a governing board for a congregation, and it became a regular fixture as the Episcopal Church took its place in the new United States of America. Even the western Catholic Church, from which Protestants had departed, has more recently been depending upon "Parish Councils" and other governance mechanisms for much of the administration in local churches in North America. In part, particularly strident lay leadership in America historically came from the egalitarian spirit that also permeated other institutions—political, economic, and social. In part it also came from the revival movement, in which such luminaries as Dwight L. Moody eschewed clerical status, sometimes contrasted their spirit-filled work with impotent "priestcraft" and European hierarchies in religion.

In local congregations among the major streams of American Protestantism—Methodist, Baptist, Lutheran, Presbyterian, and the like—lay officers and leaders have always been exceedingly important in giving direction and support. As the examples of "fencing the table" (testing by elders before communion) and the Sunday school demonstrate, lay leadership historically has balanced that of pastors and support staff personnel. Especially in rural and county seat churches, matriarchs, patriarchs, and extended families exercise enormous authority and leadership in determining congregational culture, proclaiming its story, and setting its mission. So both the administration and the expectations of ministry are shared alike—though admittedly often far from equitably—by lay leaders and pastoral staffs.

Moreover, lay leaders in congregations are subject to all the currents and forces of "incorporation," just as everyone else. Especially in city and suburban churches, where business and professional people form much of the fabric of community life and the lay leadership of congregations, they naturally apply many of the expectations and values of professionalism and efficiency to church life. They think naturally of church leadership as analogous to business leadership or leadership in professions. They think of giving to the church as similar to the paying of "dues" in other organizations. And they rely on paid staff to accomplish the administrative work, as paid executives and support people "staff" other for-profit and nonprofit entities. Want to add a program? Then count on adding a director or pastor to run it!

Before bemoaning this situation and blaming lay leaders for the disconnect between necessary administration and "real" ministry, consider that pastors, other ministers, and staff in churches collaborate in the process. They come from the same families, breathe in and bear the same values, and are tempted to think of growing the staff and church membership just as other organizations grow—by adding numbers and increasing professional leadership.

Obviously lay leaders and pastoral leaders need to work together as partners in congregational worship and work of every kind. Can this be done with effectiveness and excellence? How is it accomplished? In the next chapter, I consider two congregations in which all the leaders work together in administration for pastoral care.

CHAPTER 4

"Love binds everything together..."
Two Effective Congregations

I n the letter to believers in Colossae, Paul reminds them that they are called into one body. They should be thankful, and they should let "the word of Christ dwell in [them] richly." He also asks them, above all, to "clothe yourselves with love, which binds everything together in perfect harmony" (Col. 3:12–17). If the word of Christ is richly dwelling among us in a congregation, everything may still not be in perfect harmony. But in some congregations, we can see the mutual love and respect spelled out in their organization and ministry. In this chapter, we consider a large congregation and then a smaller one as we seek to locate "best practices" in church administration for pastoral care.

Staff Meeting

As they do every Monday after lunch, the thirty-person staff of White Memorial Presbyterian Church of Raleigh, North Carolina, gathers around a large table in a classroom of the Calvin Building. Scripture reading and prayer are provided first by John Brothers, soon-to-retire pastor for congregational care, who concentrates on discerning God's will for all of the worship and work of the church. The pastor for administration, Gary Fulton, moderates the meeting, introducing those of us there for the first time. After the devotions, both the second and the final items of business consist of pastoral concerns with people groups: various members of the staff talk about those in the hospital, coming and going from nursing homes, a grieving family, an upcoming baptism.

With everyone present—pastors, food service and custodial directors, assistants, secretaries, and part-time ministers—they review calendars, events of interest to the whole group, and special needs foreseen in logistics. Support staff leave, and the pastoral and program staff proofreads together both the church newsletter and the bulletin for Sunday. They check signals on worship and correct errors of time and spelling. "We're changing the way people take communion, so we need to announce it twice," suggests Lisa Hebacker, incoming pastor for congregational ministries. Topics for common discussion—new ministry areas, coordination of recycling, the offer of a light board—are treated succinctly but conversationally.

Several times in the course of the meeting, someone—the children's minister, the outgoing pastor for congregational care, the director of the weekday school, Danny Dieth, who leads youth ministry, and Art Ross, pastor—thanks individuals and groups for their good work. Typical is Ross's "Nice planning, nice communication, nice follow-through" to those who led the teacher education event the previous Saturday. Jane Wilson, associate pastor for Christian education and nurture herself had stepped in to provide some emergency childcare. Duly noted. There were also frequent and gentle asides among all those present, sometimes a question and sometimes a humorous comment on the topic.

The program staff leaves, with pastoral staff (including interns) staying for a third part of the meeting at which they treat remaining items on the agenda, mostly matters of pastoral care—especially the naming of all those who joined the church in the past year, each name eliciting some comments around the table concerning their assimilation into the church: "She is singing in the adult choir." "They are only in town part time." "I saw him at early service." Each name also elicits some action by a staff member. "I'll get ____ (an elder) to see them." "____ lives around the corner. I'll drop by." The meeting adjourns informally, consuming about 75 minutes in all. Pastors leave slowly, several pairing up on particular things they will lead together.

Impressive is the attention of the whole group to the contribution of each person and group represented. Here is a conscientious and spiritually mature team of leaders at regular work together. This impression carries forward into all the other activities and conversations in classes, worship, and outreach observed as the officers and members of this congregation live out Christian commitments.

White Memorial Church

White Memorial began in the 1940s, a natural, suburban offspring of downtown First Presbyterian. Thoughtful elders guided the early meetings, and they saw to it that numbers of women and young people were among congregational leaders long before such inclusive styles of representation became popular. And as suburbs became part of the city, with further suburbs and even exurbs soon far beyond, White Memorial took on the work of the city alongside other major congregations. The church grew by leaps and bounds, despite its having precious little parking, an early pastoral scandal, and other hurdles to overcome. Especially under the long-term ministry of Ed Pickard, who led by instinct and dogged pastoral goodwill, it became a multi-thousand-member church by the mid-nineties, when Art Ross was called to lead it. Today its membership hovers right at four thousand, with "clean rolls" and a higher than average percentage of members in weekly worship attendance and leadership of various programs and ministries. Mature leaders in the congregation share the work, but they readily defer to a strong coterie of younger ones who lead most of the committees.

The congregation now occupies a campus of five major buildings—the sanctuary, the Luther Building (with fellowship hall and dining area), the Knox Building (with a gym), the Witherspoon Building (with offices and library), and the Calvin Building (with rooms for classes large and small, and a chapel open all day every day). In fact, all the buildings have some classroom space. The congregation has also purchased a home nearby for use by a nonprofit for rehabilitation of previously incarcerated men. The buildings are well-lit and clean and exude evidence of frequent use.

The extensive *Manual for Operations* indicates that an Administrative Committee of the governing body, the session, has responsibility for "the care and use of all church property, all matters pertaining to personnel; publicity both within and without the church;

the preparation of statistical reports; and other administrative responsibilities of the church." Its subcommittees include: Building, Church Roll, Food Service, Historical, Inquirers and Candidates (those seeking to become ordained clergy), Neighborhood Relations, Nominating, Personnel, Property Use, Publications, and Radio/Video/PA. The person responsible for oversight for each subcommittee is named as well. But it is also evident from the manual that every committee bears considerable administrative responsibility, and all committees and chairs are responsible for communicating with all the rest. So-called feedback loops are amply in place.

White Memorial has it together, it seems—with almost everyone involved treating the myriad items of administration and the scores of programs as opportunities for pastoral care, usually in teams. Twelve mission trips this year were led by teams—to Haiti, South Africa, Poland, Northern Ireland, and Russia. All of them involved staff, young people, and adults working together. Other mission efforts, Sunday worship times, and educational programs are likewise planned and carried out in teams.

The pastors explain to me that search processes for pastors and directors of programs almost ensure that those coming onboard will be faithful Christians, team players with strong zeal for mission and worship. Lay leaders have been setting that tone forever there, and recent pastoral leadership has honed the expectation. There are three levels of interviews: first with a search committee comprising lay members and a pastoral staff person, then with a wider range of church leaders, and finally with all pastoral staff who can attend. After the interviews, the group evaluates the candidate. The positives come first, then concerns and issues where more knowledge and exploration are needed, followed finally by objections that generally impede any further consideration of the candidate.

They provide a recent example, the call of a new minister of music. They chose Karl Zinsmeister not only because his leadership of choirs has been extensive and superb, but also because he considers his work a ministry first and foremost. "While most people would think of a director of music as responsible for leading choirs, my philosophy of sacred music has been concerned with the musical expression and worship participation of the entire congregation." He entered readily and constructively into the staff meeting discussions, though he had been on staff only a very brief time.

A strong partnership among pastors and competent lay leaders seems to make the work and worship of White Memorial very special, not just in the selection of staff but in every aspect of church life. Elders lead all the committees—on education and nurture, congregational care, outreach, worship, administration, finance, and stewardship (they separate those two). Elders also form "mentor groups" for pastoral staff; work in selection of benevolences; evaluate program, staff, and themselves; and oversee the spiritual growth of the congregation. Deacons oversee the congregational care in partnership with elders and pastors, and so frequently hospital visits, care-facility visits, and home visits are done by church officers, Stephen Ministry participants, and pastors. All of the work is carefully coordinated, and an operational manual is a resource for all.

Art Ross, Pastor

Art Ross seems particularly gifted in leading a church. He attends to significant matters of administration with care, and he seems intuitively able to separate the significant from the trivial. He explains that elders and others in early congregations taught him both to engage administration thoughtfully and to gain wisdom for future ministry. Lay leaders, on the other hand, say Ross has taught them good practices. One from a church Ross served twenty years ago saw him recently and said in my presence, "Art, I'm still making one-page reports with a positive recommendation at the conclusion."

"That's the way I still ask committees to report," Art responded to my question. "I ask the chair to have a one-page report, no more unless absolutely necessary. And I ask that the report contain matters of information, considerations for the future, and recommendations for action. If a committee can ration the actions called for and produce one for each meeting, that's better than a bunch at once."

Such direct instruction concerning report style, according to Ross, frequently helps keep committee chairs from engaging in personal criticism of others. "I was hurt in a previous church where issues seemed to become personal very quickly," Ross continued. "A counselor there told me repeatedly that I either had to get tougher, or I would wind up meaner." He said he felt terribly discouraged until he learned better to work through conflict and difficult issues more openly and assertively. Now Ross frequently will say, "This is what I think and how we should decide. Convince me that another way is better." And as the attention to proofreading the bulletin and news-letter attest, he came to pay lots of attention to administrative detail as a vehicle both for group building and for modeling excellence in work and worship design.

When he came to White Memorial, Art Ross found the *Manual of Operations* that had been adopted by the governing body during the interim between regular pastors. He asked to rewrite the manual, and then the body adopted his new version. It begins with some denominational statements about local churches, but then it states clearly:

> Organization and administration fulfill a purpose, name-ly, to further the proclamation and growth of the gospel of Jesus Christ. They are a means to an end, never the end itself. Yet, sound administrative principles and practices allow the church to fulfill its mission both efficiently and effectively. Mission always determines the form and structure of the organization and administration of the church.

"I'm convinced that burnout is not a matter of working too hard," Ross mused. "It's a result of continued frustration at the inability to handle conflicts constructively. If you don't come out of conflict constructively, it sucks all the joy out of ministry."

In addition to honing abilities to resolve conflict constructively, Art Ross spends considerable time with others in peer learning groups and educational events. He meets regularly with several pastors of large congregations. He belongs to a Rehoboth Group with fourteen others pastors and educators, selecting, reading, and discussing current works of fiction in convivial settings. This considerable ongoing education would seem also a kind of Sabbath for him.

Thus Art Ross understands that congregational administration, done well and accomplished together with many others, actually contributes to his own spiritual health as well as opening deeper trust and more effective pastoral care for the congregation and the wider community. And he shares with others what he has learned about ministry, while continuing to draw upon the insights of colleagues. For as we have already seen, all the pastors—in Christian education, formation, music, and the rest—are part of a team at White Memorial. Two of the associates especially are charged with engaging administration as pastoral care, Gary Fulton and Lisa Hebacker.

Gary Fulton

For almost a decade, Gary Fulton has served as an associate pastor in charge of administration, and more recently he has also been overseeing outreach with two program colleagues. He came in 1998 from serving as an associate pastor in another North Carolina church, and his role would probably be termed "Executive Pastor" in most such positions. "White Memorial is not much into titles," he says approvingly.

He handles most of the obvious administrative responsibilities—overseeing shuttle services from two distant parking lots, for example, and securing traffic control officers for Sunday services and special events. Liability and property insurance, coordination of maintenance on the buildings, supervision of personnel assessment, and criminal background checks on employees are part of his portfolio, too. But he also shares as a member of the pastoral staff in the visits to hospitals and the counseling with officers and members of the congregation who ask for help.

"I love the eclectic job I have here," he declares. "So many people are working together for ministry and mission. I also appreciate the mutual support a number of us in similar ministries provide for one another across the country." Along with a group of executive pastors and administrative leaders in large congregations, Fulton attends an annual gathering for learning and fellowship. This group also freely shares information and insights throughout the year.

Fulton points to some additional ways the church is organized to nurture and care for members by incorporating into the community's life their piety and insights taken from mission trip journals and annual stewardship devotional guides. From a mission trip to Russia by ten members, including Gary, extracted sections from the daily journals were gathered for a "Mission Journal" and shared with the entire congregation in printed form. The entries spoke of the work, learning, helping, worship, and sights along the way. They also spoke of the faith of those involved, both visitors from White Memorial and their Russian Christian hosts. The Stewardship Devotional Guide for 2007, a pamphlet of fifty daily meditations, scripture citations, and prayers by both young people and mature members and officers spoke of death and life, work and worship from very personal perspectives. A ten-year-old told of helping a friend; an older man told of being taught as a fifth grader and now teaching a fifth-grade class how God's promises are sealed by the Holy Spirit. In these and many other congregational efforts, the circle of leadership is ever expanding at the church.

Lisa Hebacker

Beginning now to lead the pastoral care team at White Memorial, Lisa Hebacker says she is extremely impressed with the depth and breadth of systems at White Memorial, but she thinks even more important is the extent of the personal concern of so many that care be constructive and effective for members of the congregation and for those beyond its bounds who are in need of it. Before coming to White, she had experience in several other congregations as a pastor and as member of pastoral staffs. "I've seen nothing before like this," she joyfully reports.

> First, the session assumes real responsibility—not just in title. Deacons work very hard to care for people, families, and groups of members. They relate it to the nurture we provide. Then we have a group of Stephen Ministers— all trained in helping and referring those in need of more extensive counseling. We have four "Grief Workshops" a year for those who have recently lost loved ones. And we have Jim Tubbs [a retired pastor who does visits each week], who is great! There is a Samaritan Counseling Center, and we are related to it. A young seminary graduate will soon join us for part-time work while he continues education in pastoral care. On and on goes the list of good things, all needing oversight and administration. My primary job, though, is to care for people and for groups of people—administering as necessary to get the job done well. We believe passion should not outrun process, but process should not stifle passion.

She and John Brothers, who is retiring from the staff, spent two full days discussing particular needs of individuals. They listed all the areas of discussion for Art Ross to see, together with questions for him for the ongoing ministry. Their work includes administration for Services of Healing and Wholeness, soliciting leadership for "Care for Older Ones," processes for deacons to visit in homes, projects to offer "time off" for mothers of young children, a vibrant singles' ministry, ways to superintend and direct care for weddings and funerals, and many more particular functions and programs that are for the most part led by lay people and assisted by church staff. In each case, Lisa and John, with a copy to Art, looked at the primary purpose, invariably fostering a Christian practice and offering prayer and nurture in the faith.

Local Wisdom

At White Memorial, the pastors frequently employ various aphorisms and sayings that have arisen from the quarterly retreats the team enjoys. "That's what the wisdom literature in scripture really is," Ross explains to me. "It's the faithful looking back to make sense of experience so the future can be better. That's how you get proverbs." "Passion cannot outrun process; and process cannot stifle passion," "Money follows members in mission," and "Strong committee work makes good meetings," are just three of them. "Passion cannot outrun process; and process cannot stifle passion" was first used in my presence by Gary Fulton. He was talking about the development of each year's major mission emphasis. "Money follows members in mission," Lisa Hebacker said, as she told about that phrase being used time and again in the building of budgets each year. Ross used "Strong committee work makes good meetings" when he was talking of another institution, but it was recited several times in the process of interviews at White Memorial.

Trinity

Not all the churches that "have it together," seriously engaging congregational administration as a matter of pastoral care, are large ones. In fact, just as most of the Christian congregations in the United States are relatively small, so most of the really good pastoral care seems to take place as members and officers in small congregations naturally assume leadership and work harmoniously with pastors and other (frequently part-time and volunteer) staff. But many of the complicated matters for any nonprofit organization in today's world challenge smaller churches especially, and one good way of making smallness work in one's favor is to openly expect and invite all the members to higher levels of commitment and discipline.

So it is with Trinity Church in Harrisonburg, Virginia, a town of forty thousand that is home to James Madison University (about eighteen thousand students), not to mention other schools and a Mennonite seminary. The pastor of Trinity, Ann Held, served another "high-threshold church" (where every member is expected to participate fully in the mission and work) before being called there in 1990. She was open to share leadership of worship and meetings in the hope that others might be attracted to effective congregational life.

The church building is a nice old house, from 1829, several times refurbished, with additions as wings added more recently. Most people in town know where Trinity is, for many groups meet there and the community outreach of the congregation is pervasive. A governing body of twelve, its session—with Ann Held as its moderator—is also the administrative and pastoral core of the church. In a denomination that has been losing members during the past decade, Trinity has grown from 90 members when Ann arrived to its current size of 152 or so, with some more who worship there and share in the mission efforts but are not members.

Trinity does not advertise its numbers widely, as do so many of the larger churches in the city. Rather it says in its mission statement, "We believe that total commitment is the realistic command of Christ Jesus for discipleship, therefore God calls us to a life of disciplined spiritual growth that includes worship, nurture, fellowship, and mission." Among other statements, the mission statement also asserts "that 'success' for God's church is not measured by statistics and budgets, but by losing itself in concern for God's world," and that therefore this church "seek[s] to reverse the world's view of the church as an institution pulling in, to that of an organism reaching out."

As a high-threshold church, its organization is much more complex than that of most churches, notably involving much more administration than usual. But the influence of the pastor, the officers, and the members of the congregation are also disproportionately stronger in the community than one would suspect in such a small congregation.

A visitor to Trinity Church Sunday worship is invited to speak up or to be introduced by a member, then receives a loaf of bread from a member and a "low-key visit" if possible early in the week, together with a letter from Pastor Held later that week. This well-oiled program of hospitality is rather typical of every aspect of this church's life together. The organizational patterns shift, too, as new members provide gifts and the lives of others shift with passages in life. Particularly well-administrated house churches comprise the work of this congregation. One such is the Africa House church.

The Africa House Church

"When you join Trinity, you really make a commitment," Beverly explains. "Almost everyone joins a house church, and there mission and care come together." On a Wednesday evening, twelve members and officers gather in the home of Isabel Dotson, a ninety-year-old member. This house church focuses on partnerships and mission effort with African congregations. The group shares a potluck supper, reads scripture, and prays together. They talk briefly about the concerns of various members, including Joanie who has cerebral palsy and is assisted by other members of the group to eat and wheel her chair. One of the leaders, Teresa Harris, relates her experience of taking a group of students to Kenya and South Africa. "There's no better way to study early childhood development than to be deeply involved with children from another, very different culture." She laced the report with glimpses of videos of the African partners she had met—some known from their stays at James Madison University or Eastern Mennonite Seminary there, and others from the trips to South Africa by members of the house church themselves. She also mixed in plenty of wit: "We got all the students to go to the service by promising them shopping afterward—one religious experience after another!"

Several elements in the house church meeting were notable: the moving, fluid leadership of the group in which everyone took some responsibility; the accommodation by everyone to the physical limitations of the host and the handicapped member; the participation and leadership of the pastor; the level of knowledge among the members of both scripture and of the situations of a whole range of African people and communities of faith; and the careful organization that underlay the spontaneous and intimate worship, fellowship, and learning time.

Congregational Organization

"Each house church has four leaders," Pastor Ann Held explained as she served salad. " At present, Trinity has six house churches as well as regular congregational worship and governance—African Partnership, Friendship, Bridges to Non-Violence, Health Helpers, Kara (clothes closet), and Restoring Creation. They focus on providing clothes for the needy, on sustaining God's creation, on health issues, on nonviolence, and on the special needs and resources of older persons, as well as on partnership with African congregations and care for African students in town.

Trinity began in 1962 with conscious attention to the New Testament witness to church organization. The organizing pastor and seventy-seven charter members, in the words of their welcome brochure, "caught a vision of small group ministries meeting in homes midweek, gathering at the church house on Sunday for renewal, and going out into the community again on corporate mission." The pattern has prevailed, and now those seeking to join spend six weeks in study together before becoming members—a disciplined course of study describing the varied activities and the ways administration takes place. "We focus on stewardship of time, talents, and money," Isabel told me. Others said she had long provided real modeling of discipleship, taking an African student into her home for semesters at a time, giving generously from her meager resources, going to South Africa herself ("at a spry eighty-two," one participant quipped), and continuing to host monthly meetings and potlucks when she could no longer get to meetings elsewhere.

The current panoply of offerings for house churches may change soon, for each fall the congregation gathers to discern whether to make another one-year commitment to a particular house church. Some dissolve, and new ones begin each year.

"I think Trinity had the first AIDS Awareness and Support church group in this part of the state, even before most folks knew the disease was spreading to this area," Beverly mused. "It began when a new group of folk with HIV-positive relatives asked to use our building. We started a study group and soon had a house church focused on HIV/AIDS."

Ann Held

A remarkably productive and unassuming pastor leads Trinity. Ann Reed Held went from seminary in 1978 to a large congregation in Memphis, Tennessee, as one of the first ordained female Presbyterian pastors serving a local congregation in the Deep South. Subsequently she served as associate pastor of a high-threshold congregation in Memphis. She has specialized in Christian education, but her skills are apparent in every ministerial function. She has written church school curriculum and study materials for mainline Protestants broadly, and her books—*Nurturing the Seeds of Spirituality* and *Keeping Faith in Families*[1]—focus on Christian practices of piety and witness.

A highly gifted administrator, Ann does not call attention to the administrative tasks; and, in fact, she deprecates her abilities in that area of ministry—a smart thing to do, it seems, from her experience at Trinity. She does several things in much the same fashion as Art Ross: She repeats mantras of participation by officers and members, lets the governing body make decisions and backs them whether she personally agrees or not, and participates in a number of church activities not as a leader but as a supporter of other people in leadership.

Ann also accepts and articulates the unique culture and history of Trinity. She seeds ideas and lets them ripen most of the time, rather than pushing personally after making suggestions. Additionally, she participates in a number of community organizations, and she lends special leadership and networks to get some important ones underway. She explains that responsibility for everything at Trinity begins with the session of the church.

The Session

"The session at Trinity is large for the size of the church, almost a tenth of the congregation; but the work of members of the session justifies the numbers." Ann Held explains that every one of the teams and each of the house church groups are represented in session.

The Pastoral Care Team has two active members of session, one elder not serving right now on session, and two members of the church. Trinity also has twelve "Shepherding Groups" that provide pastoral care in times of members' needs. In each of those groups a "shepherd" takes responsibility for about eight "units" (families or individuals). Some but not all of the elders are shepherds.

"Just last week we learned that one member's mother died," Ann recalls. "From the church office, we phoned that shepherd, who could get word to others to keep the member and her family in our prayers. They also took food, I think."

Pastoral care is a vital part of session meetings as well. When Trinity began meetings with a devotional time, they would then "do business" and then talk together of pastoral matters in the congregation. A session member suggested turning the agenda around, which they have done. Now the meeting begins with the naming of pastoral matters, a time of prayer, then the "business," and finally a devotional time for "sending" church leaders to lead in congregational worship and mission.

The session oversees distribution and collection of sheets each September that ask members to pledge their "Time and Talent Commitments" for that particular year. All members, including children, receive such a sheet, and all are requested to pray and respond honestly and generously. On Dedication Sunday, each member offers time and talents, and also makes annual pledges of money. Of course "many churches use the idea of time and talent commitment," one area superintendent explains. "Trinity actually uses the results to good effect." Members of the session take responsibility for collating those time and talent offerings. Lists are quickly provided for the various teams concerning the willingness of members and officers to contribute: "cook a meal" goes to Fellowship, "read scripture for worship" goes to Worship, and so forth.

New members' classes are under the direct supervision of the session, with elders teaching class sessions and then giving examinations to the prospective members. "This class right now has ten members," says Ann Held. "We may make it eight weeks long, since so many of the folks are coming from other parts of the church—Baptist, Catholic, etc. Ordinarily there is a session member in charge, but several of us are sharing that job while the normal leader is out of town awhile."

Common Characteristics

These two healthy congregations, in different ways, make use of the best in worldly wisdom, but their identity and their Christian expectations of nurture, mission, and relationships are not exhausted in paradigms and current practices of management, leadership, education, or corporate life. Both congregations seem to be *in* but not *of* the world.

Congregational leaders read appropriate materials on leadership and put into practice some of the insights—from experts on communication, systems theory for human communities, matters of organization and administration. But they also discern lessons from the Bible and from Christian tradition that inform their life together.

In both churches, pastors do not hesitate to lead. Neither do those in other positions of responsibility in the congregations. Ann Held speaks of "seeding ideas" and letting them come to fruition, or not, with equal trust in the officers and members of the church. A new house church can simply appear, as sufficient numbers and energy from the congregation bring it forth. And each year, leaders together measure whether to maintain the groups for ministry and mission.

At White Memorial, Ross is prone to tell the session or the staff, "Here is my thinking on the matter. I will gladly explain my thinking if you wish. If you have a different idea or insight that goes another direction, convince me and us, and we'll go that way." Again, the common wisdom saying "Money follows members in mission" indicates that everyone at the church has opportunity to put forth ideas and mission efforts and get backing for those that draw others.

Again, both congregations work with redundant systems, groups, and programs that overlap in providing coverage, double- and triple-covering for both administration and care. That redundancy is particularly remarkable in the life of Trinity, where so few members accomplish so much. In several areas of church life to be explored subsequently, evidence of overlapping ministries and shared responsibilities assures effectiveness. In neither White Memorial nor Trinity did anyone express resentment or even concern that others might be engaged similarly to their engagement. On the contrary, people spoke gratefully of the similar work of others.

Both congregations have distinctive cultures from inception supporting shared ministry, particularly valuing the contributions of lay leaders. In the image conjured by Browne Barr, many geese take the lead, and none is afraid to honk from behind.

When James Hopewell began to explore congregational culture, he found that "parish life . . . was a rich and multi-layered transaction that seldom got the description it deserved." He marveled that "the life of each was like a fascinating tapestry woven with distinctive values and outlooks and behaviors, each telling its own pattern."[2] It might be more difficult to shift the culture of a congregation that is not accustomed to leadership from many collaborative sources. But it can be done and has been done, as further examination will show in chapters 6, 7, and 8.

In both White Memorial and Trinity, leaders were aware of impediments to effective administration for pastoral care. Several folk at White Memorial and Trinity suggested focus on what they termed "temptations," "seductions," and "obstacles," inhibitors that get in the way of good administration for pastoral care. So it makes sense to focus on that topic, before exploring other congregations.

CHAPTER 5

"Lead us not into temptation…"
Temptations in Ministry

According to Luke, Jesus told the disciples "When you pray, say: 'Father, hallowed be your name . . ." (Luke 11:1–5). In the Sermon on the Mount, following Matthew, Jesus said "pray then in this way: Our Father in heaven . . ." (Matt. 6:9). The passage we know as the Lord's Prayer continues with "Lead us not into temptation," which in the New Revised Standard Version is translated "And do not bring us to the time of trial." As the first disciples knew what it means, so do we.

Just as planning and organization, administration and follow-up have always accompanied life in the church, so church leaders have consistently been plagued by times of trial and temptations in the doing of them. Congregational leaders are not spared the trials and tribulations everyone else confronts. Scripture records early church leaders recalling not just the glaring encounter with Simon the Magician trying to purchase the power of the Holy Spirit, but also occasions on which leaders were impatient, angry, and unfair with one another, talking but not doing "the word," and so forth.

All of the pastoral Epistles, what Frances Taylor Gench calls "the dirty laundry of the Bible," deal with trials and temptations in ministry of many kinds.[1] The letter of James, for instance, treats lack of faith; showing of partiality in ministry; speaking too much; doing too little; being selfish, envious, or boastful; practicing illicit sexual behavior; lack of patience; and a host of other shortcomings among Christian leaders. First John urges us to love one another, but it also confusingly says we need to "test the spirits" and calls other believers the "Anti-Christ." Things there seem poorly organized rather than inspired and orderly. Reading James and 1 John, it seems a wonder—a miracle—that the church even made it to the next generation![2]

And the miracle continues. It seems White Memorial and Trinity pastors, staff, and lay leaders are able to put it all together well in providing for Christian work and worship today. Members of the staffs and officers of those congregations chafe at the idea that they "have it all together," however, and they readily point to ways in which they need to improve various administrative systems for church life and caring. At both churches, and most of the others I studied, leaders named seductive tendencies and personal temptations. Nevertheless, one can see the work of the Holy Spirit in their midst. Why can't every congregation be so transparent to evidence of God's healing power?

Further, many congregations are giving close attention to needed, complex matters of church administration and management. Maybe the gap between administration on the one hand, and witness, mission, and care on the other is being bridged, the problem being met.

Yet despite this apparent progress, church leaders continue to succumb to many temptations. Students of congregational life note increasing numbers of churches losing their sense of mission and vision, and becoming dysfunctional in their operations. Rather than going away, in many churches such problems are growing.

Sadly, sometimes church leaders are either not conscious of the problems, or they are unwilling to make the changes that will permit church management and administration to be focused primarily on pastoral care. In this chapter we will look at a few of the major seductions that characterize life together today. Insightful books by others treat such major matters as sexual integrity, honesty in financial dealings, and other more obvious issues for pastors and lay leaders, so here I focus instead on some of the particular temptations connected with administration and organizational behavior.

One brave member of a ministerial staff, when he heard of my wanting illustrations of leaders being tempted, volunteered to speak of his experience.

"You know, I burned some bridges and missed some opportunities for pastoral care because I wasn't paying attention to administrative tasks," Danny Dieth confessed in the course of my study of

White Memorial. A young man who serves as associate pastor for youth and their families, Danny has been highly praised by others on the church staff and by folk from other churches in the region. He leads youth conferences and mission trips well, as colleagues attest.

As we talked subsequently, Danny pointed to his gifts— for ministry with people, both one-on-one and in groups. "What I don't have naturally, and what I have to work on, are skills in communication that is not face-to-face, and in thinking ahead to plan carefully for events." By all accounts, he works well in overcoming his human limitations and natural inclinations, but he suffered from, and says he still suffers from, the unintended consequences of neglecting administrative tasks.

Danny's shortcomings are universal. His assertion, "I wanted to serve people, not paper," could be ours. "What I did not realize at first," he continues, "is that written communication and advance planning affect the quality of what happens in the events." As a youth minister, he deals extensively with families—especially parents—and with young people themselves. Doing administration effectively and budgeting the time appropriately, in Danny's words, "builds the trust and opens the time for the young people with God and God's will for them." It also builds trust with parents.

Danny Dieth led youth on eight mission trips last year. He leads an informal worship service each month especially geared for youth, which is attended by a hundred or more people of all ages. He superintends the confirmation classes that continue for eighteen months at a time. "We have one class still going, and we have another beginning with seventy-five young people in it!" he exclaimed. "It is extremely important to answer e-mails regularly and promptly and to write letters with our eyes on the Gospel. These are precious times for young people and their parents. At a conference recently I heard that two things are particularly important in order that young people claim Jesus Christ as their personal savior: time for youth with their parents to focus on the Christian faith, and occasions for mission trips or camp experiences to have a real effect on their souls."

Danny says that his determination to change—to pay closer and careful attention to the planning, organization, and communication in work—came from feelings of disappointment in a previous church, from his own will to build trust and relationships by practicing better personal discipline, and from finding at White Memorial people who were straightforward in supporting him as he overcame his weaknesses.

"We found someone to assist in some of the details," he says, "but more to the point they provide me with balance by making allowances to permit me still to relate to others personally first and foremost but then also calling me to account for ways I still need to improve." The fact that he attends carefully to it now means his ministry is more effective at the church.

Temptations Come in Clusters

Danny Dieth phrased nicely several of the temptations in ministry when he said he wanted to serve people, not paper. He realized that his inattention to communication, preparation, and follow-through resulted in losing some opportunities to do ministry and deepen relationships. He also recognized his need for others' help in offsetting his limitations. And he needed people telling him when his administration—planning, engaging the program, follow-through in assessment—fell short of expectations. What are some of these seductions that so often "lurk" like fowlers setting traps (Jer. 5:20)?

I Serve People, Not Paper

Here is one example of the problem addressed by this study—that caring for paper (or e-mail or text messages) interferes with care of people in church leadership. Truly, the work in reports and newsletters, budget reconciliation, and letters to enlist or charge members and officers with responsibility can all be daunting. A session member in a medium-sized church who had been out of town for two weeks showed me her mailbox in the church office—absolutely stuffed with letters, catalogues, circulars, flyers, index cards, and bulletins. "We were out of the country. You should see my computer!" she told me with a wry smile.

Inattention to Communication

Closely related to thinking one just serves people and not paper is the seduction of thinking that sending information alone is communicating, or thinking that communication is someone else's job.

Most of us realize from personal experience how frustrating it is to have missed meetings or decisions because we did not hear of them. When someone says, "But I told you!" it provokes all our defensiveness and not a little self-righteousness.

The opposite may tempt as well—failure to ask both about events and people in the church and about whether our own communication is satisfactory.

Thinking of the receiver in communications, and making as certain as possible that reception has been attained, opens occasions for pastoral care and deepens relationships in ministry—no question about it. Sending communication that honors, nurtures, and invites reciprocal conversation is even better.

Assertiveness in inquiry and initiating information loops is equally important. The weekly newsletter at Third Presbyterian in Richmond, Virginia, is even named "The Loop," and it contains a regular invitation for people to ask for and send information to the church office.

Linda Hay, church business administrator for ten years at St. Peter's Church on Long Island, said she raises this priority with everyone in the seminars she teaches. "Is your church office a clearing-house for reliable information? How do you stay in the loop?" she asks. She reminds us that it is equally important to keep all church leaders in that loop: "Some administrators say they are reluctant to ask the priest or vestry about things. It's a temptation to let things go, and you can't do that with communications."

"Solo Pastor"

That infelicitous phrase, "solo pastor," proves a seduction not just for pastors but for everyone involved in congregational leadership. Danny Dieth did not mention the temptation by name, but he certainly repented of having failed to gather alongside himself those who could supplement his work and offset his deficit in some gifts for detail, for example.

Associate pastors, directors of music or education, elders and deacons may all be thoroughly tempted to "go it alone." Committee chairs may suffer the same temptation. But it is particularly the case in smaller congregations, where the pastor is the only full-time employee. Even knowledgeable writers succumb, as David Canada writes in *Spiritual Leadership in the Small Membership Church*. "The pastor as spiritual leader must be able to articulate a vision," he asserts. "Through preaching, pastoral care, teaching, administration of the sacraments, and administration of the church program, the pastor expresses his or her vision."[2] Better would be the mutuality expressed elsewhere in his study, of the officers and other lay leaders being together with the pastor in conjuring, articulating, and implementing the vision for the church's mission. At least Canada includes "administration of the program" alongside pastoral care and other aspects of ministry.

While particularly tempting in a small congregation to think one person is the Lone Ranger leader, it muddles ministry and impedes ministry in a congregation. (Even the Lone Ranger had Tonto!) Our family some years ago had the misfortune of sharing worship and work in a larger congregation where lay leadership and pastoral teamwork had been a hallmark, when a new pastor arrived as "Head of Staff," or so he claimed. He wanted all significant matters to cross his desk for decision making. The associate pastors, music director, Christian educator, and church administrator soon found other churches to serve, the youth program deteriorated most rapidly, and lay leaders began to move to other congregations by the dozen. When he left only three years later, the church had been halved in active membership, and its ministry in the community was but a shadow of its former self. Our children led us to another congregation where they could participate in youth mission trips.

While some situations are not so obviously costly in discipleship and worship, the solo pastor temptation can wreak havoc in other ways as well. One of the more persistent seems to be the shunning of critique. Frequently this temptation is phrased (or implied) as "my way or the highway." Among flying geese, the parallel would be to leave behind those who "honk from behind."

Distance Dissent

It is so tempting and so human to exclude those who differ. A pastor or lay leader who seeks to go it alone may well feel threatened when a variety of alternatives is presented for a congregation. In most urban and suburban contexts, lots of other congregations are nearby. Might the person or family "honking from behind" fit in better elsewhere? Some analysts of congregations in the 1970s rather radically suggested that growing churches ought to stifle dissent, to offer a homogeneous home for people elsewhere forced to cope with pluralism and relativism. Such behavior seems terribly human, but Jesus calls us to a different way of being, a way that we have seen in some of the churches profiled.

Remarkable is the concerted administrative attention at Central Presbyterian, Trinity Presbyterian, and many of the congregations profiled toward actively seeking out various and divergent ideas and points of view. Session members at Central even pointed out that in naming the strategic planning committee, Gary Charles actively nominated people "with a wide variety of commitments."

These churches also keep asking, "How's it going?" and they make formal assessments. Those transactions mitigate another temptation.

Assessment Can Wait

At White Memorial, Danny Dieth and all staff members receive regular, annual assessments, and their weekly staff meetings are occasions for critical conversations. Moreover, in that congregation, people feel comparatively free to speak up if they sense any administrative impediment to ministry. Sad to say, few possess the gumption of White Memorial to build in evaluation strategies to the administrative expectations. Some pastoral staff members say that the most difficult parts of leading are having regular opportunities to hear from others ways in which the work and worship can be improved and practices that inhibit effective care of members and officers, and particularly to pay attention to the voices of those less vocal in the congregation.

Critical assessment is extremely difficult to hear, and in many congregations there are deeply ingrained habits in place to avoid it. As a result, some members may speak negatively to friends but not confront lay or pastoral leaders. Others may simply fade into the woodwork, finding extra time to drink coffee and read the Sunday paper. Still others, voting with their pocketbooks, may continue to attend but fail to give, or give little of their time, talents, and money.

Of course the best assessment is that which occurs instantaneously—in a spirit of freedom to disagree gently on the spot or to point to better practices or interchanges. Danny Dieth has learned to ask about the feelings and thoughts of others as he engages in ministry. According to colleagues, he invites assessment. This is an administrative matter, purely speaking, but it immediately opens relationships for pastoral care in every direction. He opens himself to critique, and he "organizes," in the fullest sense of that word, remediation and partnerships with others. It is a team-building question.

Temptations are not limited to those Danny discovered in his early ministry. A number of others plague congregational leaders and deserve our attention. In the words of T. S. Eliot, these seductions may seem "to measure out [our lives] in coffee spoons" in comparison to the major sins—apostasy, marital infidelity, theft from the church, or killing the hopes of people. But in fact, the clustering of such apparently minor temptations does contribute to major dysfunction, if not unfaithfulness itself, in congregational leadership.[3]

This Church Is Mine

We human beings love to possess things. Theologically, we know we own nothing, especially as portions of the body of Christ. That does not stop us from "puffing our resumes," so to speak. James Cushman, a volunteer at Trinity and previously a pastor of small congregations and a presbytery executive in areas where many solo pastors serve, says this insidious temptation to fraudulent self-delusion comes to almost everyone serving. In solo situations, it can be most subtle and pervasive, for many people do label a church by its pastor's name. "This is Rev. Jones's Church"; "We belong to Alice Little's church"; or "Father Jernigan's church had a supper."

Cushman explains that the worst part of the temptation is that it undercuts the work of the laity, especially the officers and leaders of the congregation. A pastor or another who thinks it is his or her church will doubtless also bear heavy stress and ultimately implode. So, in effect, it produces a negative "double whammy," undercutting both the pastor's real authority and the power for leadership among a cadre of officers and members.

Honestly, however, lay leaders can succumb to the same temptation, especially those leaders who consider themselves indispensable. Several times, I have seen a lay leader seek to have all the authority and even refer possessively to the church as "my church." With natural "matriarchs and patriarchs," women and men of longstanding leadership and wisdom, the step from "stewardship" to "ownership" can be almost imperceptible but nonetheless insidious.

In both of these instances—the false sense of proprietary ownership by either pastor or lay leader—the saying that I heard most recently from Cornel West suits well, "The peacock struts because it can't fly." The image of high-flying geese, taking turns being in the lead position in order for the flock to make the most progress possible, seems the perfect contrasting guide.

Jim Cushman, considering tempting sins, also considered the other side of pride—indolence and excuse-making.

My Dog Ate My Homework

Quite familiar with small churches, Cushman says that many pastors in such congregations also make excuses instead of simply owning up to mistakes. "Those in small congregations are generally quite willing to forgive if the pastor simply says, 'I'm sorry. I goofed.'" But Cushman has also known those who keep making excuses for mistakes and errors, frequently the very same excuses, and soon congregational leaders weary of the transactions. And the church does not have to be a small one for excuses to mar team-building.

In considering Christian practices, Thomas Hoyt claims telling the truth to be a part of testimony. "Testimony occurs in particular settings—a courtroom or a church—where a community expects to hear the truth spoken."[4] He speaks primarily of testimony as a part of the worship service, to be sure. But an excuse, especially one that blames another, scarcely fulfills the requirement of truth-telling. And in the fascinating relationship between authority and responsibility, anyone in formal authority is vested with responsibility to avoid making excuses—to tell the truth.

Majoring in the Minors

It is likewise tempting to give the newest demand of the day priority over everything else. Equally, we can easily lose perspective and think of the projects, ministries, and people in congregational life as merely a series of successive "tasks" of equal significance. In these circumstances, even the simplest prioritizing of work—into items that are "crucial," "urgent," and "important" on the one hand and those that lack deep significance or urgency on the other—can increase effectiveness. Discernment among the first three—crucial, urgent, and important—yields even more accomplishment.

A friend who serves a city church explained that she consistently tries to finish or assign one crucial, urgent task first thing when she comes into the office. Then she moves to the routine matters until the inevitable interruption occurs. She also explained that on her way to church, she prays every day for those in her care, and she is certain that her "flash prayers" while driving in help her center and discern what work is crucial and urgent from what is merely important and routine.

Graham Standish points to the temptation in many churches today to think incrementally about *functions* in a congregation as together comprising its work, rather than centering on witness to the Gospel and the spiritual growth of members of the body of Christ. "In these churches," he finds that "there is little expectation that members will experience and encounter God, or connect what they do with God's purpose, presence, and power." Even when prayers and worship occur in such congregations, the expectations are minimal—not that God will empower and the Spirit will quicken faith and action.[5]

No Flow, No Joy

Congregational leaders should feel good about the work and about themselves. As a group of us shared lunch—six church business administrators in the midst of certification classes and two of us from Union-PSCE, where the classes were held—our conversation turned to "flow." One of the students, who served as administrator of a Catholic parish, said he thoroughly enjoyed portions of his work. In particular, he enjoyed composing and sending letters of appreciation for the gifts from parishioners. He tried to personalize the letters, and sometimes he lost track of time as he engaged in this fulfilling task. An admirer of the works of Mihály Csikszentmihályi,

I told my tablemates about *Flow*, a brief recounting of his psychological studies of "optimal experience" as recounted by pilots, competitive athletes, and musicians.[6]

Conversation turned to testimonies as different participants spoke of joyful aspects of their work. Naturally, different administrators found flow in different portions of their responsibilities. One woman even spoke of her love of working with the numbers and finding them congruent. "I love it when they come out right," she told us.

That conversation some years ago, as well as subsequent listening to leaders of congregations speak about happiness and drudgery in their work, convinces me that many people resist finding this flow or particularly intense happiness in some special work.

Danny Dieth, in speaking of his ministry, said that when he saw the whole of a program or intervention in ministry, he felt really fulfilled and satisfied. He speaks and acts joyfully, losing himself in the mission effort and in the relationships with young people and their families.

To talk in more theological terms, Thomas Currie recently wrote *The Joy of Ministry*. Currie explores the "gift that issues in a certain boldness of spirit" that comes in ministry of various kinds. Personally, he finds the work of preaching most joyful, but he allows for others in ministry to sense the gift elsewhere in work. According to Currie, "The misery of mainline Protestantism today is not best described in rounding up the usual suspects of declining numbers of members, a smaller place in the religious marketplace. . . . Rather what describes the true pathos of our situation is a certain joylessness, an inability to lift up our hearts in response to the risen Lord, who invites us to participate in his victory over sin and death."[7]

Currie remembers Karl Barth remembering Martin Luther remembering that a donkey was called upon to carry Jesus to Jerusalem. "Feel your ears," Luther advised, "and you will find a lovely pair of big, long donkey's ears." Currie says that Luther used this homely admonition to warn against any feelings of self-importance. Barth "is even more right that God has uses for such donkeys, and that being a donkey with this burden brings with it a certain contentment, even a joyful freedom."[8]

Although their treatments of flow and joy differ considerably, Csikszentmihályi and Currie have in common the hope that people today will experience deep happiness and find meaning. Currie particularly shares his passion for the Christian Gospel in the midst of what he terms "the hard work" of ministry. Although neither joy nor flow is guaranteed in congregational leadership, especially in the work of organizing and following through administratively, it seems a shame if the work is joyless, if it gives little occasion to "lift up our hearts."

Currie advocates prayer and other Christian practices to locate and receive the joy in ministry. It occurs to me that these practices are tried and true antidotes to others of the temptations enumerated. Perhaps it helps to examine congregations in which flow and joy are evident, where teamwork and good communication foster excellence in a number of areas of administration, where good administration in turn opens and deepens pastoral care in the congregations and more widely. It is to this that we turn in the following chapter.

CHAPTER 6

"Glad and generous hearts…"
Governance That Grows Leaders

We Christians look to the idyllic view of the first community of believers for inspiration in our life together. We always have done so. The Acts of the Apostles tells of witnessing awe and miracles, sharing in all things, spending time in worship, and constantly praising God. These are powerful, biblical criteria for assessing administration in congregational leadership.

> Awe came upon everyone, because many wonders and signs were being done by the apostles. All who believed were together and had all things in common; they would sell their possessions and goods and distribute the proceeds to all, as any had need. Day by day, as they spent much time together in the temple, they broke bread at home and ate their food with glad and generous hearts, praising God and having the good will of all the people. And day by day the LORD added to their number those who were being saved. (Acts 2:43–47)

Through the ages, this beautiful portrait of what came to be the church in which followers shared life, and prayed and worshiped together, and to which new disciples were added, has been an attractive vision and sometimes a goal for the church. It led the desert fathers, Saint Benedict, and other founders of religious orders to fashion their worship and work. Protestant Reformers, Christian utopians, Socialists in the eighteenth and early nineteenth centuries, and many others followed suit. It gives a wonderful, compelling image of church life for today, or at least what it might aspire to be. Granted, subsequent stories in Acts show this harmony and mutual love did not endure. It nevertheless can be a goal for our organizing and care within the fellowship, and the example from Acts shows that such a common life draws new believers into faith.

Can we focus congregational governance in such attractive ways today? Can meetings and governance draw officers and staffs into deeper relationships with Jesus Christ by the work of the Holy Spirit? Can others be drawn into service by the examples of pastors and lay leaders working harmoniously? Can congregational leadership lead to generosity and praise of God? Churches that "have it together" seem to have effective formal and informal practices that meet these criteria, or at least point in these directions.

Central Presbyterian Church

Take the case of Central Presbyterian Church, Atlanta. Everyone interviewed there spoke of challenges in becoming more faithful in sharing leadership, providing outreach, evangelism, and mission. However, it is apparent from being with the congregation in worship and meetings that wonders and signs are accomplished, that they are together, and that they praise God with generous hearts. While they do not hold "all things in common," their giving for church mission and for more than a dozen affiliated ministries far surpasses contributions in most comparable congregations.

Central Presbyterian Church is one of those congregations that took the right name. Born of a split in 1857 among members and officers of Atlanta's First Presbyterian, Central met in City Hall while its edifice was constructed across the street, where the Georgia State Capitol now stands. A number of mayors, commercial magnates, and their families belonged to the church, which was spared from the fires set by Sherman's Union Army in 1864 but was not spared from the economic woes of the Radical Reconstruction years. The congregation was soon plagued, and almost imploded, by a pastor and session committed to disciplining "sinful" members and officers. People were denied communion for dancing, card-playing, perceived drunkenness, gambling, and other notorious "worldly amusements."

With the departure of that pastor, the ministry of another in the 1880s who sought nurture rather than punishment through church discipline, and the constructive leadership of its session, Central flourished. A new and elegant building on land purchased across the street from the original was dedicated in 1885. More significantly, the church made room and provided care for various "sinners"—a woman who bore a child out of wedlock, a man prodded into a duel, a young man previously convicted of intoxication. At the same time Central undertook outreach in Atlanta and more widely. Central Church bought property and established missions, Sunday schools, and chapels in various parts of the city.

Martin Lehfeldt, longtime lay leader, credits an earlier lay leader, John J. Eagan, with selfless devotion to education and mission. According to Lehfeldt, Eagan instilled the progressive mission in the common life of Central and attracted like-minded leaders in business and government to join him. Its membership grew to almost five hundred by 1900, and its Sunday school under Egan's leadership was the largest in the denomination, at 1,350. Through thin and thick, the lay leadership of Central shared power with the pastors in decision making and administrative work.

In the twentieth century, Central continued the patterns of praying, giving, and witnessing to the gospel, leaving behind the earlier fractious regulation of behavior. A commodious Sunday school building built in 1905, leadership in progressive government for the city, pioneering in race relations, support of labor unions, chapels throughout the city, a baby clinic that blossomed into a full-blown ministry for the urban poor—all characterized the ministry of Central. In the 1930s, under the leadership of yet another superb pastor and a strong session, Central decided to stay in downtown Atlanta despite the fact that most of the members now lived in suburbs to its north. A strong pattern of membership visitation, an excellent educational program, and dignified but intimate worship with fine preaching were seen as ingredients in sustaining a city church against the tide of retreat from urban challenges.

In the 1960s and after, public life in America and among Protestant Christians was characterized by divisive issues concerning race, parity of women in church leadership, war, economics, and "social activism" in general (but particularly inclusion of gays and lesbians in church rites of passage and in leadership). In this pivotal era, Central became staunch in upholding a liberal and progressive stance, at the cost of some members' participation and support.

Today it numbers about seven hundred, including several ministers and educators who attend but cannot officially "belong" to a local congregation. Its program and budget, however, more closely resemble the work of a fifteen-hundred- to two-thousand-member church because of the generous involvement of members and officers in so many mission efforts. Programs closely affiliated with the church include a child development center, an outreach and advocacy center, and a night shelter center for homeless men (in partnership with the nearby Shrine of the Immaculate Conception).

"People have told us for years that they join Central because they want to engage in mission," said Martin Lehfeldt. "So with the commitment there, and with so many talented folk, we ask for a 'Time/ Talents' inventory when people join and annually thereafter in the spring. We take it seriously and we use it. It's like the pledge of money that is likewise important in the fall. Government for us is so important. Central's long-standing tradition of outreach has been amply matched by Gary Charles's introduction of a much more theologically grounded style of government."

Gary Charles

Gary Charles loved ministry at the Old Presbyterian Meeting House in Alexandria, Virginia, where he served for more than a decade. A congregation of about eleven hundred members, it included the governor, numbers of other political leaders, staffers for members of Congress, and entrepreneurs, as well as professionals in many areas and a fascinating mix of homemakers and retirees bent on mission and activity. His spouse, Jennell Charles, started and led the first federally funded Community Health Center in Northern Virginia. Both possess creativity and discipline—a good combination—and they both have a good sense of humor.

Other churches failed to lure Gary from his ministry in suburban Washington, D.C., but Central Presbyterian succeeded. Gary sensed the call to be from God. He and Jennell joined the vibrant work of an already a well-established tradition.

When Gary came as pastor in 2004, he met with multiple small groups from the staff, the congregation, the session, and as many members as possible. He learned that many people felt committee meetings and the long session meetings were sapping the energy at Central. They also noted that many of the older members had burned out after years of faithful service, or that their work in outreach ministry seemed to bear little relationship to the organization of the church for ministry. New leaders were not emerging to take the places of those who grew infirm or who could or would no longer lead.

Gary listened as people told of the difficulty in making decisions. "There would be a motion to spend fifteen thousand dollars from restricted endowment funds on the furnace boiler, for example," he explained. "For members of the session to make an informed decision, the members would have to ask all kinds of questions about boilers, endowment policies, and contractor bids; and still they would be frustrated. Granted, we spent time on necessary matters, too, but a lot of the discussions were about matters relatively insignificant for governance." Clergy staff, especially the pastor, were spending enormous amounts of their work time in meetings each month. At least 30 percent!"

Gary took advantage of his "honeymoon" period to propose changes in the way decision making took place, most of which were swiftly approved. He requested a reduction in the number of members of session from forty-five to twenty-four. He recommended reinstituting a Board of Deacons, which had been dissolved many years earlier in favor of a unicameral system. He proposed dividing the work of session into five "Ministries," replacing a former "Council" system with Worship, Stewardship, Mission, Learning, and Congregational Care. Each ministry would be moderated by a member of session, and each would include at least one member of the pastoral staff. In turn, each ministry would have a set of committees. A Council of Ministries, composed of the five ministry moderators and the pastors, would establish the agenda for monthly meetings of session and would propose an annual budget for session approval. Almost all ministries and the committees would meet on the same Monday night of each month, thereby permitting pastors and other church staff to "float" and be available for consultation.

Organization for Governance

A closer look at the committees offers insight into the work of the five ministries. The Ministry of Worship includes a Committee for Musical and Liturgical Art as well as a Committee for Sanctuary and Sacraments. Committees for Personnel, Finance, Administration, Commitment, Care for Creation, and Planned Giving are under the auspices of the Ministry of Stewardship. The Ministry for Mission comprises the Committees for Issues and Advocacy, Global Mission, and Community Ministry. The Learning Ministry embraces Committees for Early Childhood and Children, Youth, College and Younger Adult, and Adults. Finally, the Ministry of Congregational Care includes Committees of Parish Life, Congregational Life, Evangelism, and Inquiry, and a Memorial Guild.

Each committee has clearly delineated duties, many of them mixing governance with external ministry. Thus, for example, the Musical and Liturgical Arts Committee has responsibility for the church choir but also for the Central Concert Series offered to the wider community. The Administration Committee is responsible for overseeing the work of the kitchen, but it also monitors the delivery of food to the Child Development Center. Each ministry and almost every committee looks both inward and outward.

The relatively new fifteen-member Board of Deacons attends to the pastoral needs of members, prospects, and to some degree the wider community. In concert with "Parish Coordinators" for each of the seven geographical areas in the Atlanta area in which members live and work, deacons provide care. Since the population of the Atlanta metropolitan area numbers more than four million, and since some members drive more than an hour to attend church, that is quite a responsibility. With the additional supporting work of pastors, other staff members, other naturally supporting groups such as the choirs and the twenty-five-year-old Women's Studies Group, the leaders and members of Central devote a great deal of attention to an extensive and complementary program of congregational care.

As moderator of the session, Gary also reorganized and streamlined its meetings. Decisions about such detailed matters as furnace repair became the responsibility of committees, with members who are knowledgeable about the subjects being invited to contribute to the discussion. Perhaps the most significant procedural change was the use of the so called omnibus motion at the beginning of each session meeting. It incorporates monthly reports and recommendations about virtually all financial matters. "We trusted the Finance and Endowment committees to do the required fiscal due diligence," says Gary. Now it takes special action for session to engage in discussion about a specific financial issue. "And," Gary adds, "we cut at least forty minutes from every meeting!"

People were encouraged to phone or send an e-mail in advance of meetings if they had questions about committee reports and recommendations. Preparing for meetings also meant that pastors began to call committee chairs in advance, and good committee chairs called and sent e-mails to members who might have special questions. "People don't resent phone calls and e-mails with questions and opinions before meetings," one session member said. "It helps us all to get ready to act together."

In turn, these procedural alterations freed the session to do what sessions are supposed to do in the first place: praise God; lift up the needs of the congregation, the community, and the world to God in prayer; and listen to God's Word read and interpreted.

"We had all these theologically informed people [i.e., clergy affiliates], who knew and loved Central," Gary Charles continued, "and we began to ask them to lead us in worship and communion. We also asked those properly experienced to offer theological resources for committees on an ongoing basis." This deployment serves to remind each committee of the relationship of its work to the broader mission of the church, while keeping the clergy deeply involved.

A special meeting in the spring of the pastoral staff and the incoming and outgoing ministry moderators convened to select chairs for all the committees, at present numbering twenty-four. Then a "Draft Night" brought together ministry moderators and committee chairs, all of whom selected members from the congregation according to their needs. If people were chosen for more than one committee or ministry, the subsequent plenary gathering of leaders would decide together where that person should be placed for the upcoming year.

"The draft works well," concluded one of the elders. "Seldom does someone object to placement, and since it's only for a year, one can serve knowing it's not an open-ended commitment forever."

For the most part, all of these changes were well received by the session and by the congregation, though some wondered initially if work could be as competently done in the new "culture."

Christian leadership is "grown" in Central as members gain experience on committees and as committee chairs, even before they become session members or deacons. The "Time/Talent" inventories provide information about who wants to do what, and these are enumerated and organized by staff for all to see. Then committee chairs and ministry moderators select members for the next year from among those interested, and frequently names of people with many gifts are drafted for several committees. They then work together with pastoral staff to compose the rosters for the committees for the coming year. Naturally, all seek to have both continuity and change in the composition of each committee. Such a continuing possibility of new responsibilities keeps members and officers growing in competence and experience in various ministries of the church.

The Resident Pastor Program

A grant from a national program of the Lilly Endowment, supplemented by Central's own funds, permitted the church to call a cohort of three seminary graduates who serve two-year residencies as they prepare for future urban ministry. Central coordinates its selection with four other Presbyterian churches in the Lilly program—in Ann Arbor, Chicago, Indianapolis, and Philadelphia.

Each pastoral resident receives experience in the entire range of ministry at Central, and each serves as staff for particular ministries and committees. At the heart of the program is the understanding that both pastors and lay leaders are the "educators" of the residents in this postgraduate honing of skills and perspective. Each resident also has the benefit of a support team of members committed to Christian witness and experienced in planning and assessment of the work. With the support team, the residents can speak and listen, learn and grow in confidence that the conversations and assessments will remain private and personal.

Some of the staff at Central initially found it frustrating to adjust to the presence of three new and comparatively temporary personnel, but everyone came to understand how the program deepens the church witness and work, especially in leadership development.

A second cohort of Pastoral Residents is scheduled to arrive soon, and Central is already looking for ways to extend the program beyond the constraints of the grant from Lilly.

The Strategic Plan

In September 2006, the session began holding meetings in homes of members to list goals for a strategic plan for Central. In January 2007, a committee of ten was charged by the session to formulate the plan. For more than six months, they prayed together and worked to construct "theological frameworks" for the plan. The plan was presented in September 2007 and adopted by session in October.

The plan envisions Central comprising four "Communities," each of which rests upon a theological framework and includes some focus on leadership development.

The plan first describes a "Community of Worship," whose worship and work are both a response to "God's love and justice in Jesus Christ." Its goals include the framing of "meetings with worship so all church work is worshipful": promoting worship in homes and focusing upon vocation; encouraging pulpit and choir exchanges with other congregations; using media to disseminate the experiences of worship at Central; and involving an even more diverse number of members to help lead worship.

The "Community of Invitation" characterizes itself as offering "service to God." That includes "drawing on everyone's gifts and sharing gifts entrusted to us in a ministry of mercy and compassion." Among its goals are increasing participation, hosting events, establishing campus ministry, strengthening the parish system, and strengthening the training of deacons.

The "Community of Spiritual Formation" calls for honoring "the spiritual gifts of member and stranger" alike. Goals include embracing the gifts of children and youth and encouraging theological reflection for all about "current moral and ethical issues in church and society."

The theological framework for the "Community of Reconciliation" calls for loving neighbors "by shaping a civic life that provides for basic human needs, seeks just and right relationships, and pursues peace with undeterred tenacity." Goals include providing more opportunities for congregational outreach and advocacy programs, deepening respect for theological diversity both locally and more broadly, and joining environmental justice ministries.

All the areas for strategic emphasis involve leadership development. The governance document itself lists ways to accomplish the goal. Obviously, leadership development was a part of deciding the very composition of the Strategic Planning Committee and all of its subsequent outcomes. According to one elder, "Gary Charles and a few elders worked to select members who would serve well together, and they gave a slate of nominees to the session. Everyone could see immediately that it was a fair and balanced group." Pastoral leadership, a team of leaders, exercising wise decision-making instincts— all modeled teamwork and initiative for others in the process.

What Does Growing Leadership Look Like on the Ground?

What does this governance pattern yield in worship and in work at Central? Sunday worship at Central begins at 11:00 AM with announcements, such as upcoming meetings to discuss the financial plight of Atlanta's Grady Hospital, a city-wide conference on Darfur strife, and a group trying to stop the death penalty in Georgia—all occurring at Central that very afternoon.

The worship includes welcoming a number of new members, with members of the session introducing each with vignettes about their talents and work (all without scripts—an impressive sign of familiarity with each of them!). There is a pastoral prayer naming some of those in nursing homes and grieving the loss of loved ones, and excellent music is featured, in addition to scripture reading, psalm singing, and a strong sermon.

Because of the far-flung membership (some people travel as much as an hour to attend), every Sunday after worship the church subsidizes a modestly priced lunch at which some two hundred gather for food and fellowship. As a group of new members and veterans in leadership at Central sit together for lunch after worship, they speak of the way worship together focuses governance. "It's hard to snipe at someone when you've just had communion together," says Leigh Campbell-Taylor, a current elder.

As this group talks, another group works on the applications for a staff position, and yet another group discusses a funding crisis at the nearby Grady Hospital, a major teaching facility that also cares for Atlanta's poor.

Andre Williams, a management trainee at a nearby Wendy's, joined the church recently. "I'm impressed by the way everybody here focuses on mission. It's like my home church in Omaha. But it's hard to do in this big city."

Wills and Tracy Moore tell of their involvement in mission and governance. He is an executive at Medshare, a nonprofit enterprise providing medical resources for hospitals in developing nations, and she a lawyer at SunTrust Bank. She is on the Endowment Committee and the Finance Committee, and he is on the Community Ministry team. "We have Cam Murchison as a theological resource on the finance committee," she tells me of the contribution of a member who is the academic dean of Columbia Seminary and "is really good in thinking about money!" "We're impressed with the breadth and depth of experience in ministry here," he says. "Since we've been here, I've embraced work in nonprofits full time."

"Overall, the governance is very effective if not always efficient," according to Lee Carroll, another seminary faculty member who shares in life at Central. "We all know here that the church is not in business to serve itself. So we are united in a sense of mission, even if we disagree about the priorities in accomplishing mission. Occasionally there is confusion—like we have both an 'Advocacy Committee' in the church and an 'Advocacy Center' with a separate charter and budget. Sometimes it's hard to know who is advocating what."

Sunday afternoon, the sanctuary fills again as Central hosts a rally for those concerned about the genocide in Darfur. Kate Mosely, one of the Resident Pastors, is liaison from the church for the rally, and she directs traffic and cautions exhibitors to clear aisles as they set up. The full nave and balcony; the collaboration of Christian, Muslim, and Jewish clerics; the prevailing decorum; and the bountiful reception that follow all offer evidence of the competence and experience of Central members and officers in providing hospitality and direction for public occasions for advocacy.

Monday morning in late January, members of the pastoral staff communicate with and visit members and officers in preparation for the session meeting that evening, as well as for the February meeting and other upcoming events. Monday afternoon a regular staff meeting permits pastors to worship together; to celebrate a staff birthday; to check signals with directors of the pre-school, the advocacy center, and the shelter; to think together about assimilation of new members; to check the bulletin and newsletter for the following week; and to make initial worship plans for March.

Members of the session and pastoral staff meet at 6:00 PM Monday for a light supper and for worship and communion led by one of the affiliated clergy. As the meeting begins, two new members are received into the congregation. Gary Charles and the members of the session introduce each and describe their backgrounds and interests. One who joined has already been a member of the adult choir. A report from the clerk of session, John Huss, names two members transferring elsewhere and two more recently baptized. Moving to treat "old business," the session unanimously adopts the omnibus motion for the meeting, one that includes money to reconfigure the "Youth Suite" and money for recarpeting several rooms and walkways.

A "Special Order" leads to consideration of the 2008 operating budget and a carefully prepared, unvarnished presentation of it and attendant issues by the Chair of the Finance Committee. Questions are welcomed, even encouraged, and when consideration of personnel salaries begins, the Chair of the Personnel Committee makes the same kind of presentation. The budget is adopted after significant questioning but no rancor or evident frustration. Only the matter of pay increases for Resident Pastors provokes sustained discussion; it is evident that some members still did not understand the comparatively new program and its separate budget, partially funded with a grant.

Interestingly, over the course of the meeting, leadership passed among at least ten of the twenty-three gathered, and almost everyone spoke at one time or another. Evident also was the fact that much discussion and preparation had taken place before the meeting, and no one seemed to be "completely in the dark" about anything considered or approved.

Central grows leaders, humanly speaking, in many ways not mentioned in this brief description. Theirs seems a perspective held widely if not universally that leadership should be shared broadly, and that new people coming into leadership actually strengthen the whole body, even if they make mistakes more seasoned leaders would not make. Inquiry led to almost universal affirmation that the church tried to incorporate younger leaders—extending to a youth elder who joined in the discussions and including new members and prospects in conversation at table. To accomplish this goal, excellent communication is absolutely necessary.

Meeting the Communications Challenge

In a city church, that "communications seduction" might be particularly difficult—thinking something had been heard just because it was said or written, thinking information alone would satisfy the needs of members and even officers for a sense of participation in community decisions. It is instructive to look at patterns of communication, and even at one of Central's letters to members, to see how the challenge is being met. Assimilation and movement into leadership are targets for attention in much of the regular communication.

An upcoming celebration of the sesquicentennial of the congregation invited new members to learn about the history and story of the church, for example. Brochures that illustrate some of the high points in the witness of Central in Atlanta, as well as dates for new buildings and pastoral ministries, are placed in pews and sent to all homes. One is invited to rehearse the history of involvement with partner congregations, with the mission outreach efforts over time, and with capital fund drives.

Striking in its focus on educating and inviting new leaders is the letter sent right before the celebration. "It's here! Our Sesquicentennial is upon us . . ." proclaims the greeting. But the next paragraph calls attention to temptations to "gloss over the past, blur the present, and rose-color the future," for example. It seeks God's forgiveness and God's transforming power to help the congregation be faithful in its "great calling to serve Christ in the city and world in the years ahead."

The celebration will be the occasion for launching "Project Mainframe: Computers for Change." The letter invites people to join in the support of the program and to donate time as they can for attendant work with those learning job skills and seeking employment and permanent housing. "Give extravagantly," the letter implores, "so that those who live desperately may acquire the skills to live in hope and stability."

Some people are engaged thoroughly in the new program, while others wonder if attention to it will detract from other programs underway. Here is just one example of the tension and potential conflict with which leaders at Central cope all the time.

Analysis of Conflict and Tension

In a congregation like Central, tension and conflict may still be present, yet conflicts are seen on all sides as potentially constructive rather than as threatening unity. Leaders encourage members to participate thoroughly in planning, in worship, in broaching new ideas, and in suggesting ministries. Small groups and informal clusters of Central's members engaged in various activities generally see themselves as encouraged by others with varying points of view rather than as competitors for money, visibility, and approval by the governing body. In the words of one elder, "You can't have this many folks with get-up-and-go without some friction. Everyone wants their mission interests shared by more people. That's a nice problem, isn't it?"

Such a spirit contrasts with that found in many churches, where conflict is avoided and peace—sometimes even a passive-aggressive peace—prevails to the detriment of potential leaders. Pastor Gary Charles and numbers of the others in leadership at Central possess a wide repertoire of skills and modes of dealing with conflict. They seem equally at ease with confrontation, when necessary, as with supporting and persuading on behalf of measures necessary for the church. Charles credits the night shelter and the outreach center with teaching staff and session to be forthright and sometimes even blunt in telling others about issues and needs. "Having homeless and sometimes psychologically fragile people as regular members of the congregation helps, too," he confesses. Members who might not be welcome elsewhere are vital to the mission of Central, and they contribute to its welcoming and inclusive atmosphere.

Myers Park Presbyterian

Some other elements in growing leaders can be discerned from the life of a larger, wealthier congregation in Charlotte, North Carolina. The Myers Park Church bears some resemblance to Central, with young, energetic leaders evident and lots of attention to the goal of education and nurture.

At Myers Park Presbyterian Church, meetings of the session follow a schedule of ministry emphases, so each meeting provides time for the governing body to "wrap its arms fully around one aspect of the church." Steve Eason, the pastor, says, "We even have the opportunity to pray with the folks who are doing that ministry." A typical year offers monthly meetings on outreach, education, worship, examination of officers, denominational relations, stewardship, budget, evaluation and long range planning, pastoral care, youth, and two open meetings in which members can contribute topics for consideration.[2]

Like Central, the Myers Park governing body meets monthly for dinner and worship. They eliminated most of the voting, and the body retains the right to "redirect" any committee when the body thinks the proffered plans do not meet the problems constructively. Pastor Eason advises that effective communication is imperative, and the session as well as staff take responsibility to keep everyone informed as planning progresses.

Again, emphasis on the enlistment and initial training of elders and deacons at Myers Park elicits encouragement to work as teams with members and pastors. In the words of Vicki Garrett, an elder, "Despite feeling overwhelmed at times, in the end, it was evident that we were building a team of disciples who would each bring their own special gifts and would have to work together."[3]

Church Business

At both Central and at Myers Park, developing leaders from the congregation is the business of the church—consciously and pervasively. They devote time to thinking about people who should receive invitations to lead in various ways, devote congregational resources to apprenticeships, and celebrate their achievements. Neither church sacrifices other administrative work in the process, but the sessions and pastoral staffs are not totally consumed in the organization for present programs.

Most interesting was the patience and support given by older and more experienced leaders to new leaders—giving permission to lead, even if the first attempts of the new leaders were not proficient ones. Such an environment seemed to offer spiritual space and time for miracles and awe, growth and sharing gifts in the manner of that first congregation.

CHAPTER 7

"You visited me..."
Organizing Ministries for Visiting

Most good practices for church administration come directly from experience and only indirectly from scripture. But the visiting of members, especially the homebound and those others imprisoned (either literally or figuratively speaking), is deep in the heart of Jesus's own formula for salvation, according to Matthew's Gospel. The blessed, the righteous will feed the hungry, give the thirsty something to drink, and clothe the naked. And they will welcome the stranger and visit those in prison. In these actions, they will minister to Jesus himself, according to Matthew 25, and will consequently inherit the kingdom prepared for them.

These admonitions from Jesus in scripture are taken to heart by pastors, staffs, and lay leaders in many congregations. Because the practices of service among the needy and of hospitality are well-treated in many books today, I focus here on the instruction to visit—a topic surprisingly neglected in most books on church administration and materials on the emergent church. And as William Arnold asserts, visiting is the hallmark of pastoral care, the epitome of caring intervention.

Highland Presbyterian Church

George Rue, Elder
"Getting the right question at the right moment is a powerful thing," reflects elder George Rue as he considers the way he was drawn into

the Highland Church fabric and took on a ministry of visiting members and serving more broadly. "Pastor Jim Chatham did it first, right after we joined in 1999. He told me about the tutoring program at Atkinson School and invited me to consider it. I jumped at the opportunity, and it led into my moving to other involvement."

"He and the other pastors have a knack for matching people and the needs they can meet. I was soon taking communion regularly to Mary Rountree, an amazing lady. I went to her home, and later the nursing home with another person—sometimes a pastor but mostly another elder, and my partners varied over the years. And finally as she was dying I kept visiting her." Rue's eyes teared up and his mouth quivered as he reminisced.

> I still get quite emotional about that relationship, which came from the regular communion visits during which we talked seriously with her. It grew to a deep friendship. Cards and visits from others in the church supplemented our visits.
>
> Several of us each year took her one of the Christmas trees we decorated, and then we'd pick it up after New Years. There were lots of ways she could keep good contact with Highland. On the day she died, the nurse brought a letter for her, and I listened while another Highland member read it to her. The medical folk said she might well be able to hear, though she could no longer speak. It was a wonderful letter from a good friend, and it was a privilege to share the message of the letter with her. At the visitation in the funeral home, I met the woman who had sent the letter, and it meant a lot to her, too, that Mary might have heard her words before death. That night I met lots of Mary's friends. She was a very special person.

George Rue, a businessman, is just one of scores of lay leaders, members, and pastors in the network of care at Highland. He explained that at Highland everyone is "kind of expected" to see others outside the walls of the church building, at home and work, in small groups, and elsewhere. He believes this is one way Highland stays strong, though it is located deep in the city of Louisville, where several other congregations are withering and some have died.

George Rue visiting Mary Rountree is just a small part of at least six overlapping programs of care administered by different people and groups at Highland: communion for the homebound, the card ministry, the Stephen Ministry, the Christmas tree ministry, and the ministry for older adults. Karen Lacy witnesses to the intricate weaving of relationships among people in these ministries. At first questioning whether she should be included among "congregational leaders," Karen said she joined Highland about twelve years ago because of the hospitality it extended to her and her family. She considered herself just an "ordinary, garden variety member," but she was actually involved in several of the visitation efforts, particularly the ministry for older adults. Another staff member at the church had asked her to look in on Mrs. Rountree a couple of years ago, and she had begun to visit her periodically at the nursing home. She also loved to write the cards and deliver Christmas trees when possible. After Mrs. Rountree's death, Karen began visiting another older adult who though homebound was still vitally concerned about the gospel and its proclamation. She considered she was helping another Christian keep at the task of witnessing. Karen came to yet another event each year—a birthday party at the church for those eighty and older. Members would pick up and deliver those not able to drive themselves. "I like for my daughter to learn that life involves helping others," Karen declared. "So I began taking her to see Mary Rountree, and she tagged along to some of the other things. It's good modeling for her growth, and she loves doing it."

Karen Lacy and George Rue are concerned not only to engage in the ministries to those outside the church building, but also they do their part to foster a church-wide perspective that one-on-one relationships and small group ministry to prospective members "on their turf" is a crucial part of being together as Christians.

Highland Presbyterian Church just celebrated its 125th anniversary. Founded in the first "new" neighborhood as Louisville began to grow eastward, the suburb of the 1880s was quickly absorbed in the city itself as additional neighborhoods kept pushing farther out in that direction.[1] The few members became more numerous as that process of incorporation took place during the early twentieth century. Pastor Peter Pluene, who served from 1920 to 1948, made special efforts to be in the homes of members and prospective members frequently, according to his daughter Peg Harvin, who told about the more recent pastors as well. Pluene's immediate successor, "Benny" Benfield, pastor from 1949 until 1958, loved preaching more than visiting, so he kept the retired Pluene serving in a ministry of visiting in homes and offices. The following pastor, Henry Mobley and associate Charlie Hanna, systematized this ministry; one day they made cards with the addresses of all members, and on the floor of the parsonage divided them up into thirty-five "districts." Pastors and elders visited in districts on a regular basis, as well as visiting shut-ins and those in the hospital. Highland flourished to become almost sixteen hundred members during these years, and elders remember scurrying in the '50s and early '60s to keep up with visiting the many prospective members who visited each Sunday.

By the time Jim Chatham became pastor in 1981, having first served briefly as co-pastor with Mobley, the church had become more complex and the lifestyles of many of the younger members discouraged the kinds of visits that had characterized the church thus far. Chatham engaged in numerous pastoral visits in homes, nursing homes, and hospitals, especially for those grieving or sick; but he also encouraged programs among officers and members of the church to sustain the visiting tradition in this city church. Visits came to focus on places of work and natural gatherings of members in clubs and circles.[2]

Chatham and an associate pastor named George Spransy embraced the Stephen Ministries, a one-on-one visiting program involving careful preparations for Stephen Ministers. An initial "class" of five undertook that ministry with an equal number of "Care Receivers." Soon another larger class joined them. The Stephen Ministers undertook extensive training, then regular consultation and supervision as they worked in visiting those who asked or were referred for care. In the words of Frances O'Connor, one of the Stephen Ministers, "The relationships between care givers and care receivers soon spills over, as we learned more than we helped and as others made contact with us—now more confident and capable in caring. Not even a pastor as good as Henry Mobley could see all those who needed calls. Having the Stephen Ministries system was a great help." Ever since, the Stephen Ministries program has been led by a team, and now the team includes both pastors and elders with the credentialed training.

Chatham also excelled in fostering ministries to refugees and immigrants—the biblical "strangers in your gates"—and involved scores of members in assisting new residents of the city, whether they joined Highland or not. His work in the public arena on issues of civil rights, honest government, and public education drew new members, including several dozen from the denominational headquarters upon its relocation from New York and Atlanta to Louisville. Others, simply moving to exurbs or disenchanted with the church's civic involvement, departed. Numbers declined a bit, to about 1100, but remarkably the majority of members made the transition with alacrity and enjoyed their new extra-mural ministries. A partnership with the West Chestnut Baptist Church, an urban, predominantly African American congregation, was especially fulfilling, for it drew both white and black together for worship, fellowship, and mission work. Pastors helped form the partnerships, but they also listened as officers and members advocated programs and ways of visiting. This combination was maintained, even though new programs and partnerships evolved.

Pastors and Organized Care

The visitation and other external relationships among members, congregational lay leaders, staff, and pastors being so many and varied, this division of sections into programs that came from the tradition and those emanating more recently from concern and mission seems arbitrary and may be misleading, but it may also illumine the following systems and patterns of care.

With Chatham's retirement in 2002, Highland called Fairfax Fair, the first woman to serve such a large congregation of Presbyterians in Louisville. Fairfax is supporting the various ministries already underway while she fashions and envisions additional efforts in this direction. She suggested recently, for example, a special emphasis on apprenticeship for leadership among the many new members, as Highland is growing in numbers to more than 1,250 presently.

Everyone considered visiting members to be one of Fairfax's priorities as she embarked on leadership at Highland, though she still considers her own efforts modest in this area of ministry compared with the emphasis in previous decades. One longtime member said, "I don't see how she does it! But we love the fact that she's available, present for us, and that she really listens."

The other pastors and staff members at Highland also contribute to the various ministries of caring beyond Highland's church buildings. Joel Weible and Melissa Head, associate pastors for congregational life and Christian education respectively, both perceive their work as crucial in this area. Both do make calls at the homes of members and officers, though both said most members prefer to meet for lunch or for coffee in mid-morning or mid-afternoon on "neutral turf."

"We administer a 'progressive dinner' every so often for the young adults," Joel said. "People like sharing their homes, and this puts less pressure on anyone than would a full dinner program at one place." More frequently, Joel organizes Wednesday night suppers at the church, events he says he has to "juggle" in the city church because of the prevalence of "no-shows and walk-ins." After a modest supper, the choir practices, kids go to different activities, and adult nonchoir members study in a variety of settings. This fellowship and learning time Weible considers "of one piece" with the visiting, since both help solidify relationships. With a permit in hand to close the adjacent street, he led a "PRESFEST" (Presbyterian Festival) in the fall at which families and singles, church members and those in the neighborhood gathered for a cookout, music, and various games. "No big sell for the church," he explained." Just a welcoming time for everybody and especially for neighbors who might become part of us."

Melissa commented that visiting for youth and families of children was best couched in terms of fellowship activities—bowling events, skating together, renting canoes for an outing. "Those in the confirmation class gather periodically at the homes of members for instruction—especially as members of the class meet with their sponsors," she explained. "They also engage in projects in area nursing homes and hospitals, which are sometimes linked to members who are residents there." Melissa works on the activities at church but visits in homes as well. Especially she sees families of those in church school and those who are seeking to enlist as teachers and leaders.

Both Joel and Melissa expressed deep appreciation for the atmosphere at Highland that encourages pastors and lay leaders to get to know members outside the church buildings whenever possible. They laughed together: "Everybody warned us about the woman who insists that pastors visiting eat some of her 'special congealed salad,' and sure enough, we were both offered some when we made our respective visits."

"One elderly member here named Bob Lehman was recently telling us that though Highland's emphasis on being in homes and other gathering places might well be considered 'inefficient,' such ministry is crucial for Highland," Melissa Head recalled. "He told us that one-on-one and small group Christian relationships are the best antidote to the temptations of a consumer, me-first society."

Ministerial Staff and Organized Care

Frank Heller, who has served Highland as minister of music for more than a decade, oversees youth and children's choirs as well as the adult choir of forty he directs. He prizes the relationships among choir members and for this reason has divided the adult choir into "Tone Clusters" of six to eight members each. These clusters take turns distributing and gathering in the sheet music month by month, and they also provide desserts every so often when the fellowship occasions call for it. More important, the clusters become primary units of care when members are sick or have life passages—family baptisms, weddings, funerals, or anniversaries. Frequently it is a member of the cluster who alerts the rest of Highland to a need for visits from others in the congregation.

At the beginning of the year, members of the adult choir contribute to a fund that pays for cards to be sent to those who need contact. They are encouraged to visit one another as well, and many members and families of the choir travel back and forth together for dinners and other church meetings. Frequently members take meals to one another in times of need. Because they are in close touch in these various ways, people are more willing to ask each other for prayer as well. In terms of more overt administrative tasks, Frank coordinates the work of members and clusters by sending a weekly "ChoirNotes" e-mail message. He finds that thanks to all their combined efforts, the good morale and mutual caring extends to the youth choir and to the four children's choirs as well. Students who are members of Highland go to school all over the city and surrounding county systems, so the choir gathers young people and children otherwise not frequently together. Thus the mutual caring and the retreats for choirs are all the more important.

As do other pastoral and staff members, Frank primarily considers his work to be a form of ministry rather than a technical teaching of music or a performance-oriented vocation. When I visited the church, he was leading youth and adult choirs for the Sunday morning worship; only on Monday did I learn on Saturday night, when he had been at a youth choir retreat, one young man became ill. On the way back from driving the sick teen to his parents, Heller had a car accident trying to avoid a deer in the road. Though his car was totaled, he had nevertheless returned to chaperone the retreat until Joel could come from town to take his place. And here he was devotedly leading the choirs the next day.

While the choir offers resources for one another in a special way, Kristy Hubert coordinates care programs for most members and officers. Kristy and her family were members of Highland before she joined the staff. She found that her background as a nurse, and particularly in parish nursing, suited her work as she began to coordinate ministry with older adults. Showing me her extensive file, she said, "I developed a plan and step-by-step follow up—after interviewing everyone—for each member who was homebound." Lists are divided into categories: "Acute, Fragile, Grief Follow-up, Calls Monthly, Continue in Prayer," and so forth.

"After a good start, our Stephen Ministry at Highland had become stagnant, so Melissa and I took the training and cranked it up again." Kristy counted more than fifty members of Highland now equipped in the ministry, most still actively giving care and receiving supervision.

In response to her work and that of others in the network, a sizeable monetary gift had been received to permit older members to provide oral histories of their involvement and their memories of Highland and, more broadly, of Louisville. Kristy considers the interviews, the visits, and the network that now supports visits and care to be "holy experiences." She also points to her close working relationship with Mike Smith and the finance committee to assure that the whole church benefits from the oral histories.

Mike Smith is also involved in overseeing visits. The church business administrator, Mike said it pleased him that pastors and lay leaders at Highland took his work seriously as a ministry and not just as a necessary task of tending property, service staff, and finances. He oversees the work of an accountant and those who clean and cook in the church buildings—and some of the structures are more than a hundred years old—but he focuses primarily on church finances.

Ruth Chaffins and Marilyn Nelson serve as support for the pastors; Ruth manages the office, and Marilyn directs the media communications. Ruth and Marilyn provided some of the best insights concerning ways that leaders at Highland are able to manage and flourish in such a complex situation. Ruth, who has belonged to Highland for forty-nine years and worked on the staff for more than two decades, says that she enjoys the lack of fighting for "territory" there. "Everyone cooperates, and I'd like to see even more visiting of the regular members at home as well as those who are sick or grieving." She recognizes, however, that many people today are simply unavailable, not as in previous generations when many kept regular hours in their homes. "Back then, Dr. Mobley could simply go to any district and call on people. That's not possible today," she pointed out.

Marilyn, who has been a member of Highland "for only twenty-four years" (compared to Ruth's forty-nine) and had only worked there for four years, stressed ongoing communication among staff and members. "You can't assume people will know you," she explained. "You have to put yourself out there. We all have to do that on the staff. The only thing that really hurts programs is confusion and lack of clear communication. If I don't know when a meeting is scheduled, I say 'I'll get back to you,' and Ruth makes sure we have accurate bulletins and newsletters.

"I get as far out in front of the calendar as possible with dates and times, and I do some explaining, annotations, so people know what is involved in the event. Web folks think we say too much, but I'm convinced our reach outside the buildings is assisted by our clarity and timely communication." The staff takes evident pride in surprising people "by being Johnny on the spot." Their organizational priorities and effective administration provide timely care, which is deeply appreciated.

A Thick Culture of Hospitality

As we talked, we sensed and articulated together that Highland offers a "thick culture of hospitality." It extends to the visitor at worship, who receives a card and a phone call, and perhaps a visit from a pastor depending on the response, after a first visit by a member or officer. It continues with a focus on persistent calling and visits if someone is interested in joining. It extends to afford disciplined attention for assimilation if a person or family joins the church. "The members of the choir recruit for the choir right when people join," said Frank Heller. "I don't follow up unless the choir member asks me to call."

Even the literature and Web page on "Member Care" focus on hospitality.[3] The admonition of 1 Peter 4:8–10 is the centerpiece: "Above all, maintain constant love for one another. . . . Be hospitable to one another without complaining. . . . [S]erve one another with whatever gift each of you has received." It advertises a constantly updated Fellowship Calendar and a Prayer List of those in need.

The hospitality is multi-layered, and I did not sense any feeling of jealousy or territory on anyone's part. If more people visited someone in need, all the better! Several explained that this sense of cooperation rather than competition emanated from the pastor, the staff, and the session alike. It also became apparent that the whole congregation and especially the leaders at Highland have an expectation that everyone will "stretch" their caring among the members, wherever the opportunity permits.

Fascinating was the insight of another elder, not currently serving. Mary Henry expressed skepticism about all the programs and the "organization" underlying the culture of visiting outside the church. But when pressed, she admitted that she participates in a number of the ministries, and she appreciates many others. "I don't like the numbers—thirty-five Christmas trees, and seventeen quilts for healing!" But she recognizes that others do want to know "results," while she simply "does her thing" by visiting as many folk as she can. So, as is always the case in any gathering of humans, the multi-layered ministries at Highland healthily include critics as well as participants and administrators of programs.

Belmont Church

To have a multi-layered and thick culture of visiting, a congregation need not be large and complex. A former pastor of a medium-sized church outside Charlotte explained how the three hundred or so members and their officers and pastor worked in visiting homes and those not at church.

"At the Belmont Church there are really three ingredients in the recipe for visitation"; Richard Boyce hesitated and deliberately held out three fingers. "The deacons have responsibility. The Stephen Ministers equally care for those who are sick. And the pastor visits regularly, too." Richard Boyce has served the Belmont Church, a congregation in an exurb of Charlotte, North Carolina, for more than a decade. He is also a seminary professor who teaches preaching and pastoral care, and therefore he is particularly well attuned to the need for regular visits in the homes and workplaces of congregation members.

> You need to see people at times of life transitions—when they lose a job or get a promotion, when they graduate from a program or retire, when their kid leaves home or another comes into their home. We coordinate efforts to see that this [visiting] happens, and the obvious first need is when people are sick.
>
> The current system started when one of our deacons became a Stephen Minister. That is a good group because they train self-selected people who want to provide pastoral care. This original deacon and a couple of other members went through the training, and they started helping at Belmont. Then she saw that deacons are supposed to be doing pastoral care, too. So we organized the board of deacons so every member of the church "belonged to" someone from among them—and every so often, the deacon would call the member or visit them.
>
> Initially, we assigned every deacon to such visiting, but we discovered that some enjoyed it and some found it particularly hard. So we tweaked the idea, so that now only one group of deacons visits people.
>
> It's always a struggle to balance the emergency visits with the regular visits. I work with the Stephen Ministers and deacons so that I do some of each kind of visit. We found that if the pastor only visits when people are really sick, or if the officers only visit when the every-member canvass is going, people understandably don't let us do

the real pastoral care—neither the ordinary everyday care nor that around crises.

We trained together theologically, practicing, aiming at Christian pastoral care for the members—asking how each visit could represent the church and witness to the presence of God for those they visited. It wasn't just friendly neighbors. It was Christian ministry. I also needed help to keep from thinking of myself as the CEO of a church. My job, first and always as pastor, is to preach the gospel even when I'm listening to people.

Typically, I carry around in my head and heart the text on which my Sunday sermon will be based, and ask throughout the week what the Lord is saying to us in this passage in this situation. Right now, for example, I'm to preach on Romans 8, and we almost always take that passage as a word of comfort. But as I've been visiting around I see that passage also bears a challenge—in experiencing height and depth and angels and rulers and principalities we know nothing separates us from God's love in Christ Jesus. Doesn't that mean we, like Paul, should be encountering all those things in creation? This message of challenge, that officers and Stephen Ministers should be thinking theologically, was my "input" in the training. When I did visiting, I saw the people I thought needed visits. But I also took "orders" happily from others, went to see those I was told to see, especially by the deacon in charge of meeting the need for that person.

Lots of times people see their congregational visits through the lens of systems theory. I respect Friedman (*Generation to Generation*, 1985) very much, and I teach systems theory to officers and seminary students alike. But my primary consideration is bearing the love of Jesus to a broken world; it's what I call being a teaching elder and what you can call pastoral care in the big sense of that word.

Belmont Church seems organized in a simpler manner than Highland, but the results are comparable in making certain that members receive individual attention and regular visits. It seems that thanks to visits in homes and elsewhere, people are not caught off guard by what is happening in the church, for example when special requests for giving are needed, say for a capital funds drive or a new ministry with refugees. People expect to be visited, expect to be kept up to date on what is going on in their church community, and thanks to that they feel great ownership in their church's ministries. And when they are ill, they are not startled by a visit from the pastor or an officer in the congregation. It does not make them think they are receiving the Protestant equivalent of "last rites."

Highland and Belmont churches have had a tradition of visiting in homes and other locations away from the church facilities. What if a church less accustomed to these practices seeks to begin such a ministry?

Sunburst

At First Congregational Church of Berkeley, California, when Browne Barr served as pastor, he began to ask serious lay volunteers to work with a supervisor so visits in homes and elsewhere could be more of a regular ministry. Three volunteers began the effort, with Barr as supervisor. Then a Leadership Review Committee determined that a vacancy in the professional staff should be filled by a group of volunteers rather than by another associate minister. They advertised and solicited candidacy from competent lay leaders to secure six "sector leaders," mature members and officers who could devote time and disciplined energy to congregational care, evangelism, stewardship, and nurture. The expenses of these volunteers would be addressed in the church budget, and each would be provided an allowance for educational purposes, in addition to the covenanted education provided by leaders of the church.[4]

A search committee for the six first advertised in the church paper, then interviewed candidates to select six leaders. Leadership education for these sector leaders was multi-layered, with regular seminars in pastoral care and church management led by pastors and other professionals. Regular supervisory times were covenanted year-by-year, more intensively at first and then periodically thereafter. In a summary of accomplishments, one leader reported that after a year, each of the leaders had made contact with the vast majority of church members in that sector; knew quite well at least half of them; opened new channels of communication between the members and the church officers; reconnected some "lost" members; organized a taxi pool to get older members to worship; enlisted many members who opened their homes for church teas, lunches, dinners, and other convivial occasions; and helped new members become assimilated in church life.

This novel approach brought together various elements in church administration and oversight of members, but especially it provided for visitation among church members and linked solicitation of new members, assimilation of those who join, perennial issues of giving and volunteering, and what might be termed "deep and personal" methods of communication.

Today it seems a number of congregations employ some variant on this pattern of seeing to the care of people in their homes and workplaces—on "their turf," so to speak.

Expectations in Congregations Today

Already a century ago, pastors and other congregational leaders debated the wisdom and need regularly to visit the homes and workplaces of members. Brooks Holifield, whose work treats only pastors and pastoral staffs, describes the debate. Washington Gladden in 1907, for example, advised annual visits, but he thought church meetings were better locations to "get to know" people. Phillips Brooks did no visiting, and Henry Ward Beecher assigned assistants the task. On the other hand, Holifield says that Henry Sloan Coffin made a thousand visits per year.[5]

Today many church leaders contend that the members of "their" congregations do not want or expect visits. Others, such as Highland, find various ways of conversing with members at home, at work, and on "their turf" extremely important for congregational health and membership care. Whatever the mode of providing caring visits, some kind of hospitality and assimilation for nurture and care remains crucial in today's increasingly depersonalized society.

Indeed, the "thick culture of hospitality" found in the congregations described here, matched by their expectation that members and officers, staff and pastors will be visiting shut-ins and others at home as well as those in hospitals, seems to bear much fruit in congregational resilience, sense of stewardship, and openness to engage needs in the world more broadly.

This observation is reinforced by the findings of others, such as Kennon Callahan, who has spent his life as a student of congregational life. He places what he terms "Pastoral and Lay Visitation" as the second of twelve keys to an effective church.[6] Such visitation is crucial, he contends, in order for congregational leaders to listen to and respond to the needs and hopes of members, and crucial also in helping members to sense the mission and significance of the gospel and the church. It is likewise essential in enlisting new members of the community for its work and worship.[7] Beyond these benefits he enjoins pastors, staff members, and officers in the congregation to visit simply in order to make friends and deepen trust relationships. Callahan actually develops formulas regarding the optimal number and frequency of visits, and he suggests that the governing body of the church, not just the pastor or staff, determine how many and what kinds of visits will be best for that congregation. Groups of officers and members can then be appropriately equipped to make their percentage of the calls, and workloads of pastor(s) and staff can then be adjusted knowledgeably to accommodate the remainder.

In my experience, the pastors, staffs, and congregations that are well organized to provide visits for members, especially those in need, are not only more healthy than ones that neglect members outside the church walls but also invariably are more mature and effective in responding to all the challenges that beset every church.

CHAPTER 8

"Hearts follow treasure..."
Stewardship and Ministry

In speaking about storing up treasure in heaven, was Jesus teaching about money as well as faith? The Gospel according to Matthew tells of Jesus saying as a part of the Sermon on the Mount, "[S]tore up for yourselves treasures in heaven. . . . For where your treasure is, there your heart will be also" (Matt. 6:20, 21). Hearts follow treasure. And hearts follow money. This plain and simple statement of priorities for believers is echoed time and again throughout scripture. Your heart will follow your giving.

One of the most thorough scriptural treatments of stewardship and giving is found in Paul's correspondence with the Christians at Corinth (2 Cor. 8, 9). Paul, administrator of the "Great Collection," invites believers to join with others in helping those in need. "You will be enriched in every way for your great generosity, which will produce thanksgiving to God through us; for the rendering of this ministry not only supplies the needs of the saints but also overflows with many thanksgivings to God" (2 Cor. 9:11–12). The followers of Jesus in Corinth are invited to complete a cycle of grace begun with God's gift of Jesus, then Jesus's giving of himself, and growing through the gifts of others.

Much of congregational administration still involves money, giving, stewardship, and budgeting. Almost all of those interviewed for this book said issues of finance were among the most difficult and time-consuming for church leaders. Naturally, church administrators deal with such matters all the time, but lay leaders, pastors, and members of pastoral staffs also brought up stewardship consistently. Several of those interviewed recommended Bayside Church as a community that takes giving and stewardship seriously.

Bayside Presbyterian

"We do weekly testimonies, but we call them 'Minute for Mission,'" says Dick Keever, who has served Bayside Presbyterian as pastor for more than twenty-five years. He begins naming ways the church is organized to accomplish its stewardship of time, money, and other gifts, commenting, "We think it is important for members of the congregation—for all of us—to see the connections between our giving and our mission throughout the year."

Elders Judy Crossman and Sarah Williamson join Dick and me for lunch. Judy is a longtime member and officer and Sarah is a high school senior planning to attend the University of Virginia with a merit scholarship.

"It's natural for us to think and pray together," Dick explains, "for we do planning together both in the session and in the 'Commitment Committee,' which has specific charge of eliciting pledges and gifts each year." Dick says that "you have to change stewardship programs every few years, because ways of thinking change and because people become used to a method and less conscious of their need to give."

Judy begins enumerating programs at Bayside that are linked to giving, and the list is an extensive one: supplying a food pantry, mission trips for youth and intergenerational groups, Presbyterian Disaster Assistance relief efforts in coastal Carolina and the Gulf states, housing the homeless, Habitat for Humanity partnerships, and partnership with churches in Kinshasa, Congo, and Teciel, Mexico. "It is important for people to see the results of their giving to the work of missions," she asserts. "We become personally involved in the wider church."

Sarah explains that at age seventeen she has already participated in six or seven mission trips to Mexico and places in Kentucky and North Dakota within the United States. Youth raise their own support for such trips, mostly from other members of the church, and Bayside adults pay their own way. The pastors and lay leaders provide both the opportunities for involvement and the logistics for finance—budgeting, record-keeping, and final financial accountability.

Bayside is the most generous church in the area in meeting needs at presbytery and national church levels. Dick says that it is because the leadership keeps explaining to members of the congregation what their gifts support. "We support 'our seminary' [Union Theological Seminary and Presbyterian School of Christian Education is nearby; we were classmates there], and we support all the theological seminaries together," he says. Elder Crossman explains that one scholarship fund was initiated to honor Keever's long tenure as their pastor and to support the training of future pastors and church educators.

Dick Keever

> After seminary and a year of further graduate study, I served a newer congregation in Lynchburg, Virginia. Right from the first I was drawn to think seriously about the administration of that congregation's budgeting and finance. When I arrived, I learned that they began a budget by taking 90 percent of the pledged amounts and working from there. It seemed to me condescending to members of the congregation to "discount" the promises people made for their giving. It took a while, but we turned that around.
>
> It's been my practice wherever I served to plant ideas, then pray and work for them to blossom. I've also encouraged people to grow in giving, not just to the church, but especially to the church. No Presbyterian pastor needs to protect the pocketbooks of members of that congregation! I also encourage children and families to talk about their giving and to begin practices of giving very early in life. That's the way I learned about money and giving.
>
> Here in a Navy area, lots of military families have not thought deeply about giving in congregations. They would give a dollar a week or something at base chapel for the needy, but the government would take care of its operating expenses. Unchurched folk are even less aware of what it takes to support all these ministries, and now in Bayside we get a fair number of people like that, too.

Dick considers the decisions about congregational stewardship modes and information to be the job of the officers working together. "Sometimes all the members of the session have signed the letter asking for pledges, and sometimes they have called, or visited folk if the Commitment Committee focuses that year on some mode of canvass."

Bayside Financial Nuts and Bolts

At Bayside Church, preschoolers romp on new playground equipment. The atrium-style entrance links the educational building with offices and sanctuary. With a membership of twelve hundred, Bayside has continued to grow while most other Presbyterian churches in the area have declined. Its budget for 2008 is right at $900,000. A number of additional offerings through the year, for denominational causes, in-kind contributions, and to support mission trips and projects bring the total funding to about $1.4 million. For several years, the church has provided periodic announcements concerning its endowment, and now that fund exceeds $450,000, upon which about $30,000 is drawn each year.

Don Cannell at Bayside enumerates some temptations such as laziness and greed that can thwart the effective work of those who lead in budgeting and finance areas. One of the three lay volunteers who supplements staff work on finance at Bayside, Don is a retired Navy officer. He explains that in consultation with members of the committee and the pastoral staff, the chair of the Commitment Committee each year makes the major decision about the program to elicit pledges. Some members will not pledge regardless of the program employed, he says. For both the 2006 and 2007 pledge years, Bayside used a variant of the "Consecration Sunday" method—with members and officers telling about the various ministries and with each family or individual (or "giving unit," in his words) walking to the chancel with a completed pledge card on one particular Sunday. For several years previously, the congregation had used a "Pony Express"-type system with people taking pledge envelopes to one another in their homes and encouraging one another to "take a step up" in faith.

The committee chair decided in the fall of 2007, and the committee and session concurred, that Bayside would simply send letters inviting pledges to the work of the church. The chair of the committee felt that the change was timely. Initial letters and follow-up letters to those not yet responding yielded pledges about equal to those from last year, but fewer units made pledges. Cannell and others spoke of hopes that the Commitment Committee would stretch further in leading Bayside to more thorough giving promises during the coming months, but such engagement is uncommon.

What Pastoral Leaders Know

Many pastors, educators, and even church administrators strenuously avoid engaging the giving practices of congregational members and officers. In more than forty years of participation in congregations, and in more than three hundred congregations studied, I can count on two hands and one foot the number of churches in which the officers and members systematically challenge themselves to give generously and proportionally in a sustained, organized fashion. In those congregations, including the two reviewed in chapter 4, ministry flourishes in part because stewardship receives attention year round; and the pastors and lay leaders administer stewardship plans and expectations to help themselves and their congregational colleagues grow in faith and effective service.

These congregations, as some of the descriptions indicate, stress the giving of time and talents as well as giving for congregational support and more broadly for human welfare. Some talk about tithes, most focus on proportional giving, a few employ one or more tools from purveyors of stewardship materials, and all work together in considering congregational priorities.

Most pastors and educators with whom I have discussed giving do not know what members give, and I find their reasoning difficult to understand. Many say that knowing would tempt them to "play favorites" within the congregation. Most are concerned that their salaries are large parts of the church budget and they would be involved in a "conflict of interest." Others say it is not their business—it is not part of ministry. Still others explain that it is better for the lay leaders to oversee finances, because they are more experienced in money matters. In some congregations when I ask lay leaders, they are amazed that I even raise the question. "Of course pastors do not know what we give. Why should they?"

For one thing, according to a mature pastor with much experience, giving is an indication of spiritual health and vitality, just as are attendance, leadership, and other external indicators. Why would the leadership of the congregation not want to have this indicator of spiritual health available to them, to help determine times for intervention and presence for care? Giving, like other external indicators, might change for many reasons, such as a loss of or drop in income, fear of the future, alienation from the church, or a crisis in faith. But congregational leaders can inquire about physical and spiritual health if they know patterns and practices of giving.

In larger churches with administrators, and among treasurers in small congregations, the typical pattern is for the person who keeps track of congregational giving to protect that information as top secret and confidential. In the words of veteran pastor Ed Stock, "They play their cards very close to their chests." Several in conversation said they wished the congregational culture were more open and candid about money; but they felt the subject out of bounds in all but fall stewardship campaign season (a.k.a. budget making).

Brian Kluth

Brian Kluth, pastor of the First Evangelical Free Church of Colorado Springs and longtime student of Christian giving, suggests that the question of whether the pastor should know how much individuals give is the wrong question for congregational leaders to ask. Better is the question, "*What* should pastors know about people's giving?"[1] Sometimes pastors and other church professionals model poor and naïve personal and familial practices. It would seem difficult to engage others responsibly if one is not knowledgeable and disciplined in matters of personal finance. The pastoral Epistles in the New Testament make this point several times (1 Tim. 3:5; James 3:1–5, etc.).

In fact, all of us know of church leaders who "crashed" because they squandered resources, some even becoming culpable for misusing church funds. Financial analysts tell us much of this behavior is at least initially due to ignorance and a lack of discipline.

My long-held theory of why church professionals avoid dealing substantively with money and finance is that our calls to religious service frequently involved some "renunciation" of the world and its ways—consumerism, social ladders based on wealth, and acquisitiveness. Some Roman Catholic religious vows are explicit in this regard, but even Catholic lay leaders who work full-time in the church seem to bear the same values. Among Protestants, such values are worthy. Lives not devoted to getting and consuming, eschewing social climbing and plutocracy are certainly more susceptible to the positive Christian values—generosity, meekness, love for others, and care for creation and creatures.

Jesus was certainly explicit in calling followers to higher goals and values in life. "No one can serve two masters," he said. "You cannot serve God and mammon" (read "money") (Matt. 6:24). It is one thing to serve money, and quite another to make good use of it. When people are generous and intelligent in giving, and when they care materially for spreading the gospel and caring for the poor, they are being faithful. Wise use of money undergirds all of these enterprises. Note the conversion of Zacchaeus!

Just as in other areas of church administration, good personal practices and wise leadership for others can provide effective pastoral care for individuals and for congregations. Moreover, if a congregation embodies responsible stewardship, its teaching ministry in the community and more broadly is augmented.

One congregation, after much planning and prayer, recently undertook a capital campaign designed from the outset to devote half the money to mission and only half for its own use in refurbishing the building and adding staff. With money raised from the campaign, they opened ministry among recent immigrants, among recently released inmates, and among social service efforts in a neighborhood across the city. Such an endeavor challenged other congregations and organizations to think more broadly about need in and resources for the community. Confronting severe needs of others and meeting some, congregational leaders thought, would help set priorities for the improvement of worship and educational space needs for themselves. After all, the members of the congregation possess comparatively enormous financial resources.

Cattle on a Thousand Hills

A number of good publications address the need for church leaders to develop cultures of giving in their congregations and related nonprofits. *Growing Givers' Hearts*, by Thomas Jeavons and Rebekah Basinger, even takes for a subtitle *Treating Fundraising as Ministry*. Though it discusses parachurch organizations more than congregations, its admonitions are useful and constructive—don't use secular, manipulative techniques; appeal to altruism more than to self-interest; build trust and transparency in organizations; and the like.[2]

But again, it seems more fruitful to look first at some best practices among congregational leaders and take principles and wisdom from their experience. So in several interviews with Christian leaders, I explored ways to cultivate cultures of giving and looked at their implications for pastoral care.

Growing in Competence and Confidence: Ed Stock

Experienced, retired pastors responded with candor and good wisdom. "My competence and my confidence both grew with time, you might say." Ed Stock looked at the ceiling and smiled. "I was naïve for a long time, and the church and I both paid for it." He spoke of his experience in leading congregations in areas of stewardship and giving. "I learned to know what people give. It tells you lots about their lives and needs."

> In that first church in St. Bernard Parish, there were only six officers, and we came quickly to be remarkably candid with one another. For a small congregation, they gave well and even provided some money for mission and service elsewhere. Seminary classes did not teach me about organizing congregations, giving, and money, but that church began to do so.
>
> On the staff of Evergreen, I was able to learn from a master. Vann Arnold, the pastor, was strictly a people person. He supported the members of his staff team—

took time with them. And he knew and cared for the officers of the church, so when he needed to focus on money they were right there with him almost all the time. He didn't shy away from talking about giving, but he did it naturally, telling about budget needs and opportunities to increase ministry.

When I got to Buntyn, we decided to work hard on giving. After all, the Bible speaks clearly about the subject. We studied scripture, and we prayed together about it. We also invited a Colonel Wright to work with us, a retired military fellow who consulted out of national offices. He asked each member of the session to write on pieces of paper his or her yearly income without giving their names. Then he simply totaled the numbers and showed us what 10 percent of that would be—and what 5 percent, 2 percent, and 1 percent would be. He estimated the session represented the economic spread among the members of the congregation, and then did the numbers again. You could see some lights come on as people thought about congregational mission and program in light of increased resources.

Leaders in that congregation were then willing to go to others and say what they had pledged in light of our disciplined study and mutual commitment to mission. It was more than just teams visiting; it was a congregational Christian education effort. A few people refused to say anything about their intentions for giving. I think a couple of people even moved on to some other congregation; but the great majority became much more serious about giving, and that affected our life together. It surely offered opportunities for me to serve the pastoral needs of the congregation more effectively, and soon we had the new sanctuary paid for, and an associate pastor as well. Attendance and membership went up. But more, we were moving in mission at times when our faith was tested with civil rights issues and problems with national priorities.

Clearly, better stewardship occurred. And Colonel Wright told me I could be a much better pastor knowing what people gave. At first I was hesitant about asking. The treasurer played his cards close to his chest. So I just asked numbers without names. Soon I could deduce the names, and soon he loosened enough to tell me everything.

When I went to Second Church in Lexington, Kentucky, I noticed that the search committee members called the church "A Sleeping Giant." They had a culture of not telling the pastor about the giving of people; so I just made my pledge and asked for the numbers on the pledges from other leaders. I was amazed to see my paltry pledge (10 percent of my modest salary) was the second highest among the officers. So I raised the topic in an early meeting, and I saw another fellow get very embarrassed—a member of the search committee! Turned out his pledge was the largest, the one bigger than mine. He said outright that many folk had more money than his family, and asked what could be done. Talking frankly about money together—something they said they had never done before—helped us be open about other matters where honesty and growth were needed.

We took it from there, and soon giving was lots higher. It helped that one fellow made a challenge gift and others stepped up to the challenge. The church women's groups also began to step up their giving in addition to the increased giving from families and single members.

In the Texas church, there were lots of people who could give much more than they were. One told me frankly he would be giving 6 percent of the budget, for he thought any more than that would not be healthy for the congregation. He wanted others to do their part in supporting the church, and he worried that if he gave more he would become personally possessive of church programs and personnel. I encouraged officers to learn more about stewardship. Two elders attended a conference at Mo Ranch (the regional conference center), and one came back transformed. He had heard good presentations, and he had time to absorb the message concerning God's generosity and our response in giving. He too helped set the tone and change the culture for giving.

Soon others increased their gifts and therefore the original giver gave more. People of modest means appreciated the wealthier ones speaking openly about the ministry we could do with more money. Among the officers, we began to focus on tithing and proportional giving leading to it.

When I was called to Raleigh, I was able to lead in a campaign to enlarge the program of the church and its benevolences. Others were beginning to ask me to help their congregations also. I find that if officers are willing to pray and study together, and if people are simply honest and care about one another, they will also learn generosity and Christian discipleship better. In my second year there, we built in a criterion for the calling of elders that each was expected either to tithe or to work toward it. We had other criteria we developed—being faithful in attendance, a willingness to represent the congregation in meetings of regional church bodies and ecumenical gatherings, and some others."

Ed Stock came to believe that educating church officers was the most important part of stewardship and led to healthy and generous giving in the congregation. "Each year at Raleigh, whether the market went up or down, we had more giving than the year before as more people came on board with proportional giving and the goal of tithing," he testified. And in every interview concerning giving, congregational leaders spoke of teamwork and shared responsibility.

Craig Showalter

At the Westminster Church in Dayton, Ohio, church business administrator Craig Showalter serves as co-director of a team charged with stewardship and giving ministries. He serves with the pastor, seeing his role as providing perspective and help in peripheral vision for the pastor. At Westminster, in instituting year-round consciousness about stewardship, they have found that periodic "Faith Stories" from members, particularly those deep in the leadership of the congregation, are especially productive. "It helps all the way around," he says. "It's a testimony not just urging people to give of themselves and their resources, but it does keep that theme before the congregation."

Craig had been pastor of three congregations before concentrating on church administration in a larger, more complex congregation. At Westminster, he rather quickly gathered a working team of interested people, studied the giving patterns, and began with them to focus on ways appropriately to challenge everyone in the congregation to practice generosity. "We brought together people who were already generous and those charged with leading stewardship efforts. We didn't get everything we wanted from the church, but our patterns of giving have improved."

Stewardship Grows from Teamwork

Another retired pastor, Haywood Holderness, who had served one congregation for more than twenty years, also spoke to me at length about how good pastoral care and good experiences in teaching generosity feed each other. The church he served—Westminster Presbyterian in Durham, North Carolina—became one of the strongest in the area during his ministry there.

> I always found people ready to give, and healthy in Christian vocation, when they could devote themselves to something they cared deeply about. That is the first thing—to listen to members of the church very carefully when they speak. You have to visit them on their turf— not just in their homes, by the way. If you just see them at home with whatever family they have, your relationship will seldom extend to their vocations. And sometimes their passion is for something the church does, but another group focuses more clearly—like political reform or ecological concerns, or some halfway house for people with particular needs. I would encourage people to give their money in those directions just as quickly as something in the church.

Careful attention to the cultivating of generosity seems worth every ounce of energy invested. Dick Keever, Ed Stock, Craig,

Showalter, Haywood Holderness, and other leaders make a practice of it. They say that results show even more in the pastoral care of people than in the additional financial resources garnered for ministry. Disciplined preparation for and administration of worship likewise characterizes many congregations, including Bayside, First Raleigh, and Westminster. Administration of worship opens pastoral care and deepens it as surely as does concentration on stewardship.

CHAPTER 9

"When you come together…"
Administration for Worship

The saints in Corinth were apparently not exhibiting "best practices" in organizing worship, so in his first letter to them, Paul advised them to come together in orderly worship, bringing hymns, lessons, revelations, tongues, and prophecy. But, he cautioned, let the assembly receive the contributions one by one—not too many of anything. "For God is a God not of disorder but of peace" (1 Cor. 14:26–40).

Unruly worship! Wealthy coming early before the poor got off work and consuming the food and especially the drink! A lack of respect in dress! Worse, immorality at home! Taking fellow believers to court! The problems among those saints in Corinth provoked some of the best Christian instruction in the Bible for celebrating the Lord's Supper, for respecting each member of the Body of Christ to build up the whole Body, and for loving one another: "For I received from the Lord what I also handed on to you, that the Lord Jesus on the night when he was betrayed . . ." (1 Cor. 11:23); "Just as the body is one and has many members . . . so it is with Christ" (12:12); "If I speak in the tongues of mortals and of angels, but do not have love . . ." (13:1).

Paul addresses the requisite nature and demeanor for worship in the chapter following these three iconic passages. And of the administration of worship, Paul says, how it is organized makes all the difference in the praise to God and the upbuilding of the Body of Christ. "All things should be done decently and in order" (14:40).

Some would say that Presbyterians may have taken this summary rather too well to heart. Most have neglected to see the companion verse—permission for tongues, interpretation, prophecy, and revelations to be represented. Most mainline churches of other denominations may be in the same situation. And the so-called "worship wars" can divide even small congregations into opposing camps. In fact, I have found it tempting to consider writing a book on "worst practices," taking Corinth as one case of Christians behaving badly, and focusing on worship conflicts as the epitome of similar behavior today.

Yet today so many congregations are hearing the biblical text and countless other passages that inform *good* worship practices! They transcend the divisiveness, and their organization and administration for worship provide insight for the rest. I know two very different churches that evidence good administration resulting in excellence in worship—Third Presbyterian in Richmond, Virginia, and Old Pine Street Church in Philadelphia, Pennsylvania.

Third Presbyterian Church, Richmond

Members of the "Hospitality Team" provide welcome and bulletins for worship in a refitted fellowship hall at Third Presbyterian. Soon all the four-hundred-plus chairs are full for the 11:05 AM worship service. Mostly composed of young people and young families, the congregation sings and sways, some clapping along. Associate Minister Cory Widmer, age thirty, welcomes the congregation, and Tiffany Perry, perhaps even younger, opens the worship with a responsive reading from Isaiah 55. The band leads in several praise songs—"Unchanging," "Hungry," and "We Worship You" among them. Three guitars, two drum sets, an electric cello, and another singer lead, as the congregation reads from two simple screens sandwiching the stage.

Pastor Widmer reads from Mark 14, and then he preaches from behind the communion table about the nature of the Lord's Supper to be shared. "It is more than words. It is really Jesus present. For our past, present, and future." He stresses the heritage in Passover, the surprise when Jesus revealed his identity, the grace in providing believers everything for salvation, the joy in responding, and the reconciliation and hope in resurrected life. Congregants come forward for communion by intinction while Pastor Widmer circulates, offering the bread and cup to those who cannot easily make the circuit. An offering, a welcome of new members, prayers of the people, and a song of commitment with benediction complete the service.

The bulletin describes the service in detail, including a request to "refrain from leaving or entering the worship service during the sermon, scripture reading, and times of prayer." People obey the admonitions scrupulously, and though several score of young children, toddlers, and babies are present, these parts of the service are dignified, quiet, and well attended. The worship service moves smoothly, though leaders explain that today for the first time chairs are arranged in a more informal, semi-circular fashion. They have planned together to permit easy movement for the communion. The worship service possesses both dignity and intimacy—a friendly environment both for the young mother, baby in her arms, her toddler, and for the older couple seated in the row together.

Simultaneously, a traditional Presbyterian "Service for the Lord's Day" is taking place in the sanctuary of Third. A similar number of congregants, dressed in suits and dresses, sport coats and pants suits, participate. Steve Hartman, the senior minister, preaches, and on the same texts as Cory Widmer. What is termed "traditional" at Third would probably be called "blended" in most circles, employing a wider hymnody than typical, East Coast worship in a Protestant congregation.

Two other Sunday services have already occurred—one more traditional with communion at 8:30 AM, and another contemporary service, attracting mostly baby boomers, at 9:30 AM. Fewer attend these two services, but on an average Sunday more than nine hundred people worship in the four services at Third. With a total membership of 1,250, such high participation is exceptional.

In addition to Steve and Cory, Nelson Ould serves as executive minister, John White as director of music, Kim Taulbee as associate music director, along with directors for Christian education, preschool, lay ministries, co-directors for children's ministries, two parish associates, and the urban ministry associate, Tiffany Perry.

On Tuesday morning at 8:00 AM, everyone who has been leading worship the previous Sunday, and those who will lead worship on the following Sunday, gather for an hour and a half of formative and summative evaluation of the services. Mark Valeri, a professor from the nearby seminary and parish associate at Third, also attends regularly. Ten or twelve men and women are usually present. According to Ould, "The key is to get a lot of talent around the table and then for each of us to be a humble learner."

Those who will preach give their interpretations of the upcoming texts from scripture. The others present chime in from time to time with thoughts about the texts, the worship, the prayers, and the logistics. Ideas are exchanged freely, and the musicians focus primarily on the implications of the texts and sermons for the choices in music, though some decisions have long been in place that will center the worship experiences in scripture, themes, and church seasons. Most of the time is spent looking forward to the next Sunday and to other worship services during the week—upcoming funerals and weddings, if any, special services, and worship related to ministry efforts.

The pastoral staff I interviewed all explained that at Third they take Sunday worship services seriously, but that the worship at Third extends throughout their considerable mission and programs of nurture and care. In the words of Nelson Ould, "Everything we do we hope is worshipful, and you might say our mission is worship of God."

Steve Hartman

"Planning and administering worship at Third is a moving target," Steve Hartman reflects. "It is exponentially more complex with each additional service. What we have now differs from our practices six months ago, and six months from now things will be different from today. We assign leadership for the contemporary services to Cory and the executive pastor, Nelson Ould, who has been taking responsibility for the final integration of the traditional services most of the time. We've been in the process of changing that right now, too. It's important for me to preach in every setting from time to time, but mostly I preach for the more traditional services."

Steve, who came to Third more than a decade ago from San Jose, California, speaks easily of both his leadership and the shared responsibility for all the worship services.

We meet three times a year for an entire morning—during the summer for the September–December period, in December for the rest of the year until the end of May, and then in the spring for June, July, and August. In preparation for those meetings, I try to line out roughly the preaching schedules for each service, the basic scriptures, and a paragraph in most cases describing the themes and interface with life at Third. In the meetings we modify and edit my rough outlines in light of insights from colleagues and their knowledge of upcoming opportunities.

For example, this summer we will have a visiting pastor from mission partners in Uganda. Nelson figured out times for him to preach while he is here. We also invite the parish associates to preach, and the members of the congregation expect me to preach every once in a while in every service. No worship service "belongs" to anyone, and we want excellent sermons along with excellent prayer and music at each one of them."

Steve speaks easily about the problems and shortcomings he encounters and of the challenges Third faces. "We have this increasing presence in East Richmond, and we also want to start a second congregational site west of us. It's a stretch for this church and it affects our worship." According to Nelson, Steve's leadership style encourages lots of people to join in and share the vision. "He just doesn't have a big ego," Nelson reflects. "That means teamwork can be the hallmark of our worship planning, as for everything else. And Steve gives credit to others freely, as well." Nelson also cites the pastoral "timing" Steve exhibits. "He finds just the right thing to say to the right person to move things along strategically and to encourage leadership. He seeks quality in all our worship services."

Nelson Ould

Executive minister Nelson Ould actually came to serve at Third before Steve, and he has served there for more than a decade. Raised in Richmond, with a doctorate in pastoral theology from Edinburgh and additional study under renowned pastoral care professor Don Capps at Princeton Seminary, he came to Third to work in pastoral care and with singles and youth.

When Steve arrived and Third began a more flexible, team approach in worship leadership and planning by including musical directors, elders, deacons, all pastoral staff, and those in Christian education, Nelson began assuming more administrative duties. He still visits frequently in homes and hospitals—in fact he teaches courses at Union-PSCE seminary in the theology and skills of visiting. But he also oversees planning for worship. He shows me the agenda he constructs for each Tuesday time of assessment and planning.

He explains that he roughs out the outlines in time for the retreat meetings several times each year. Welcome/preparation for worship, confession, announcements, scripture/sermon, offertory prayer, prayers of the people (pastoral prayer), benediction, and even greeting at the door are assigned to particular people far in advance of their service. Each member of the pastoral staff takes a turn at each responsibility, and for the retreat meetings, pastors think together about the weight of responsibilities and the interests and gifts of pastors for the scriptures and themes to be addressed overall during the period. Nelson also produces an overall "Sunday Worship Planning Workshop" agenda with several particular goals, such as "Discern trends and movements of the Holy Spirit," "Advance 'fear to faith' sermon theme thinking and planning," and so forth. With a reminder to remember "multi-sensory, testimony, creativity" when planning each Sunday's worship, the agenda also includes time for theme planning, prayers, discussion of growing edges, confirming liturgists, and some singing. As a result of the assignments being made as much as four months in advance, congregational leaders can plan their own schedules in such a way that they can attend pertinent Tuesday meetings to review and assess previous Sundays and plan for worship the coming Sunday.

Then for each Tuesday meeting, Nelson produces another agenda, and he works with music staff to implement what has been decided, to keep coherence. In private, he counsels with newer liturgists and worship leaders, talking for example about how they may have assumed congregants comprehended "insider words," when they overused phrases, when they failed to speak clearly, and the like.

Nelson explains that a change has taken place. The music director is coordinating the more traditional services, and the associate director is taking additional responsibility for the contemporary services. Still, the pastor who is to preach has the final say on hymns, prayers, and of course on the sermon. "It is complex," he smiles.

> But it works like a charm. They appreciate being given overall responsibility, not just input into their parts. In fact, everyone appreciates the sharing of the work. The only parts we "restrict" to pastors are those we must— Eucharist, for example, and most preaching. Even there, sometimes elders and deacons provide portions of the Eucharistic prayers as well as take charge of the distributions. We all try to invite broad participation in worship leadership—at our best, we don't have spectators. That can produce a hodge-podge—or something really rich. We work hard for the latter.
>
> For example, there will be four different people offering "Prayers of the People" at four different services on a given Sunday. We encourage all to write down their prayers in time to exchange with the others, so by the time we pray them in worship they will have received ideas and phrases from one another.

This cooperation over the prayers of the people is just one example of the careful coordination, planning, and assessment of worship at Third.

Coordination, Planning, and Assessment

Hallmarks of the administration for worship at Third are coordination, planning, and assessment. Hartman tells of the assignments— including specific assignment to someone at each service to make certain announcements are crisp, accurate, and appropriate. The director of music is generally assigned responsibility for the two more traditional, or blended, services, the associate director for the two more contemporary services, but both make suggestions back and forth and share ideas and sometimes exchange leadership. Nelson usually works to make the more traditional services "click," checking on bulletins and making certain sufficient lay leaders are available. But the director of lay ministries selects most of the liturgists, making certain they are equipped to speak in public and clearly understand their responsibilities.

Worship services at Third include more "testimonies" now, and Steve considers these personal, confessional words from faithful lay people extremely important in connecting the worship of the congregation with its mission work. Third is heavily involved in ministries in the city of Richmond—a health care service, especially for immigrants and poor persons lacking access to regular health care; a ministry among business people; a network of homes and gathering places for teenagers in Church Hill, a poorer section of the city; and a host more. The church also joins congregations and churches more broadly in ministries and mission internationally—in Eastern Europe, in Africa, and in Latin America. The pastoral and lay leaders want to include all these concerns regularly in prayer and in congregational focus during worship.

Then the regular ministries of the church—the music, the Christian education, the work that members and officers do in their many Christian vocations—all these need attention as well. Steve, Mark, and Nelson all think the constant feedback from folk and the regular assessment of the differing services keeps everyone thinking together about the mission and worship of the church. In the words of Mark, "Nelson and Steve, now abetted by Cory, have always displayed an open, collegial, and humble spirit in planning worship and even discussing the upcoming sermon. They genuinely are open to corrections and suggestions. Real conversation marks their interaction with staff, even as they assume the final responsibility for the content of the worship service."

Third Presbyterian is not bound by its past. But amazingly, neither is one of the more historical congregations in Philadelphia. The Old Pine Street Presbyterian Church has been in the same location for 240 years, and the building resembles those of several "ancient" church edifices around it that now have become museums and façades for condominium complexes in downtown Philadelphia.

Old Pine Street Church, Philadelphia

The website www.oldpine.org announces that worship is "what we do at Old Pine." Deborah McKinley, the pastor of the 160-member congregation, explains that when she came the congregation had suffered some conflict, and now an informal theme is, "We don't want people upset." This theme, standard in most congregations and certainly in small ones, has not stopped the Old Pine Street Church leaders from organizing to enrich worship for grown-ups and children alike.

When first begun in 1768, Third Presbyterian Church in Philadelphia was located on Pine Street, on the outskirts of town in a neighborhood called "Society Hill." George Duffield, first pastor at Third, or Pine Street as it came to be known, took a leave and served as a chaplain in the Revolutionary War and chaplain of the First Continental Congress. John Adams belonged to the church, as evidently did Benjamin Rush, who also worked with Adams nearby at Independence Hall.

Its illustrious history included pastorates by Archibald Alexander, Ezra Stiles Ely, and Thomas Brainard, who led Old Pine into the New School at the Presbyterian division of 1836–38, and who served the congregation for thirty years. Brainard, an abolitionist and early prohibitionist as well, helped the church grow significantly during his pastorate. The churchyard and cemetery, given with the land for the church building by Thomas and Richard Penn in 1766, contains the graves of over fifty Revolutionary War soldiers, at least one Tory, a signer of the Declaration of Independence, and scores of professionals, craftspeople, and their families. The surrounding blocks of townhouses, commercial establishments, and other churches grew with the city.

Meanwhile, over the course of the nineteenth century, Third came to be known as "Old Pine Street." Additions to the building in the 1830s allowed for more pews, and in the 1850s provided space for meeting rooms and a Sunday school—all during Brainard's pastorate. Also redesigned in Greek Revival style of the mid-1800s, the building sported a distinctive, high-pitched roof. It could seat about six hundred at worship.[1]

Philadelphia grew during the nineteenth century far beyond any edge at Society Hill. In fact, as suburbs grew in the first decades of the twentieth century, the neighborhood declined in population, and buildings, including Old Pine Street Church, deteriorated. Participation dwindled in other Presbyterian congregations in the vicinity—in fact, First Church of Southwark, Scots Church, and the Mariner's Church all were eventually merged with Old Pine. The congregation maintained a ministry for immigrants, and for a time offered services in Polish for the few new Polish Americans in town who followed Reformed worship.

Rather than close the church, Presbyterians in the 1950s organized the "Friends of Old Pine" group—Christians who mostly belonged to other churches but cared to keep Old Pine as a vibrant as well as historic church, to renovate and reinvigorate work and worship there. They also located and secured money for location of the Presbyterian Historical Society and a community center in the same city block, in what is known by Philadelphians as "America's most historic square mile." Gradually, thanks to the Friends of Old Pine, renovations occurred and the walls were stenciled with Christian symbols and reminders of the three churches now one in Old Pine. In the 1990s, a Steere and Sons pipe organ was installed as well, a nineteenth-century instrument restored by a competent organ aficionado, Patrick Murphy.

In 1971, Old Pine called William Pindar as pastor, and he had a creative ministry and helped the congregation regain its legs and discover its mission. He sometimes engaged in a "clown ministry," for example, something that appealed to many in those years. The congregation grew during his eighteen-year tenure and continued to grow during the two-year service of his successor, Joan Salmon Campbell. And the reinvigoration of the neighborhood of Society Hill at the same time brought an eclectic cohort of professional people and young families dedicated to urban life.

Deborah McKinley

Deborah McKinley began as pastor of Old Pine in 1995, and Thomas Faracco in 2001 became director of music. Together with a Christian educator, a church administrator, a director of operations, a seminary intern, and custodial staff, they comprise the paid leadership, while a session of twelve and a diaconate of twelve supply lay leadership for the congregation. McKinley, whose spouse David Rich is also an ordained minister and enjoys helping as a volunteer, understands well the subtle administration of worship, and she considers excellent worship as the partner of sacrificial Christian service in the world. "I was sought and called to deepen the spiritual life of the congregation and to help them grow in commitment, and numbers if possible. By the grace of God, it seems we are growing in both."

She speaks of the distinctiveness of worship in a small congregation.

We usually have ninety or a hundred there on a given Sunday. The sanctuary space is such that while it's certainly not full it seems pleasantly populated, and we don't "rattle around" either. We begin worship at 10:30 AM. People are not looking at their watches all the time, and sometimes worship is an hour, but more often it's seventy-five minutes—sometimes even ninety minutes. There is a suspension of chronological time. We are caught up in *kairos*, or holy time.

We follow the Reformed "Service for the Lord's Day," with movement from call to worship to hymn of praise to call to confession, confession, assurance, and passing of the peace. The scripture readings are usually from the Hebrew scriptures and the New Testament (an Epistle and a Gospel reading). The Psalms are sung each week. We frequently have anthems between readings. Right after the singing of the Psalm, we have a "lesson for young Christians," and then those from three to eight or nine years old are dismissed to Sunday school.

At times, I've tried preaching at the communion table or the font, or even down in the center aisle; but I'm constantly using my notes or manuscripts, and it made more sense and is more comfortable for me to use the pulpit. After the sermon, our affirmation of faith, and a hymn, we have a time to express joys and concerns. Then one of the deacons will offer the prayers of the people. I believe Old Pine is unique in using the deacons in this leadership role. The office of deacon is one of "sympathy, witness and service." The deacons are people who call the community's attention to the intersection of the suffering in the world and the compassion of God, so their liturgical function should reflect this particular gift and leadership.

The worshipers come forward to make a financial offering, sing a song of praise, usually one verse of a hymn, and then a prayer of thanksgiving is offered.

The benediction follows, and then we introduce visitors and have church announcements. A dismissal follows announcements.

When we have the Lord's Supper, we either serve it in the pews or, for those who can, we come forward from the pews and receive it by intinction or take a common cup or individual cup—all offered up front. We even use a silver chalice for wine and a clear crystal one for grape juice. We also serve juice in individual cups. All the people receive in the ways they want. It's just one part of our consumer culture that keeps impinging on a counter-cultural experience.

The church devotes concerted attention to training in and education for worship. The choir—about twenty on a good Sunday—is an especially gifted one for such a small congregation. They practice regularly on Thursday evenings, and they can be anchored with professional voices in sections because of financial gifts for music. "The section leaders are part of the choir, not performers for it," according to Thomas Faracco. Other choir members practice and train as well, and so do all worship leaders—the deacons, for example, in order to lead pastoral prayers, and the lay lectors who read the scripture lessons.

"When I came," Deborah remembers, "the deacons did whatever nobody on the session wanted to do."

We worked together to change this so the deacons were tending to appropriate responsibilities—to give them worship responsibilities in accord with the serving mandate of scripture. We worked a whole year on that among the diaconate. One thing for them to learn is that you don't have to pray for everything and everyone every time by name. They learn to pray for people in nations at war, rather than naming each location of hostility. Some pastors have that trouble too. Some deacons were not willing to pray publicly and even now some demur and we honor their reluctance. But gradually most have come to flourish in their special responsibility.

I lead in the expressions of joys and concerns, and we've worked on that as well. Now almost everybody simply briefly names the person and the reason for their joy. When we started, there were lots of issues with people saying much more. Now when someone does more than just Christian name and condition, I recite back in the microphone for all to hear the abbreviated version. And the deacon is taking notes, then praying for all of us.

Over time, having different deacons pray gives us a prayer repertoire that is richer and broader than one person can do. Last Sunday a deacon, an immigrant from El Salvador, prayed for the places from which we all come. We had a visitor from Indonesia, and I thought about the special meaning of this prayer form for that newcomer to America and to our church!

Deborah speaks knowingly of "managing the necessary tension in Christian worship." People ought to feel the disconnection between their lives and their freely chosen obligations as the redeemed, for example. So those really at worship sense their unworthiness at the same time that they sense faith, hope, and love. This chasm between reality and Christian aspiration makes for a natural tension, and it is the leader's responsibility to manage it rather than seek to dispel it. She sees that in a small congregation the overall responsibility for vision belongs to her, even though it is shared with lay leaders and others on the staff. The Worship and Music Committee is not always of one mind, and some are still reluctant when change is introduced. McKinley says she tries to "listen, listen, be patient, and listen" when people have objections. "Now that I've been here more than a decade," she says, "I can anticipate when someone will feel negatively about something coming up. I can call and alert that person before the meeting of session or the worship service. Dissenters, on the worship committee for example, feel they have been heard even if they do not get their way."

She also speaks of "managing hospitality" as a major administrative responsibility. "We have visitors every single week for worship," she says.

We have to keep a careful balance in a little church like ours between "welcome" on the one hand and "counting" on the other. We need to be warm but not look too hungry, like we are desperate for new members. We ask visitors to introduce themselves after worship, and some folk always take extra care to go speak to them.

People newer to the faith feel like outsiders when they seem to be the only ones present who do not know all the words to confessions and prayers. The bulletin tells people where to find the Apostles' Creed, for instance, in the hymnal; and I always open the hymnal when I am leading our affirmation of faith. We don't want newcomers to feel alone in reading it. We also make announcements about the worship service itself at the beginning, and try to double up in communicating.

Managing communications about worship is a part of the administration of worship, she believes. "People think in such a small church that everyone will know everything, but we don't or we forget. Before the Easter brunch for the neighborhood, someone might stand and simply say, 'We need hams.' I know to explain cryptic announcements just as I abbreviate prolix ones."

Deborah laughs remembering a recent problem. A capital campaign had been launched to buy new carpeting for the sanctuary. After a session vote one night, the contractor removed the carpet the following morning, so she sent an e-mail to the congregation to prepare them for the change in acoustics. It meant worship came with a big change and only scant warning. It was a challenge in ministry, and a challenge administratively.

Deborah McKinley spoke respectfully of the others who regularly lead worship, especially of Tom Faracco, who directs the music and plays the organ.

Thomas Faracco

"I've been working in churches, with choirs and music, for many years," Tom Faracco says with a smile. "This is the most agile and open congregation in terms of worship that I've had the privilege to serve." Tom, who chairs the voice department at the Westminster

Choir College during the week, came first as an interim in music and quickly decided he would enjoy Old Pine permanently.

> Deborah and I meet several times a year for several hours at a time to coordinate the worship several months in advance of the actual services. She follows the lectionary in preaching most but not all of the time, and she brings in plans for scripture texts and sermon themes. I bring possible hymns and anthems based on the lectionary, and then we discuss together ways to make the different aspects of each service fit together and also fit the liturgical season as well. And the Worship Committee meets periodically, mostly to discuss recent worship times and offer good assessment.

Tom compliments the congregation on its ability to learn new hymns and to contribute on key gifts of exquisite Christian music to the congregation, for excellent worship.

> We employ Taizé chants some during prayer times, and frequently we will sing a verse of a hymn in transition from one part of the service to another. The choir is quick to learn new music, and people in the congregation do not complain if things are different in worship.
>
> When I first visited Old Pine, they had a dramatic reading of the Passion narrative for Palm Sunday, interspersed with hymn verses and brief anthems. I loved it, and it's a kind of tradition now. But this year we will offer a cantata on Palm Sunday, and everyone is okay with that as well.

Change and Continuity

Congregational leaders at both Third and Old Pine say openly, perhaps even brag, that their churches are open to change. None of the pastors or lay leaders interviewed speaks of change for its own sake, but they indicate that worship is excellent because their church cultures permit improvement when necessary.

In the words of Tom Faracco, "The people give us leeway to offer wider, deeper ways of praise and prayer." According to Steve Hartman, the officers and members at Third have grown in their ability to trust new forms and patterns of worship, in part because the church tries to appeal to different age groups and believers. Nelson Ould considers Hartman's inviting and open style a major factor in Third's growing into better organization for worship.

In both churches, the pastors and the pastoral staffs are working with others to help the congregations move adequately into the future. Both church staffs consider excellence in worship crucial for achieving their distinctive missions. Both balance the admonitions of Paul to worship decently and in order, with room for the work of the Holy Spirit and the joy and celebration that praise of God entails. They balance dignity and intimacy. Finally, both pastors and pastoral staffs "let go" while they lead, to share participation among the wide array of members and officers as congregants.

It seems apparent that the quality of congregational worship is enhanced as pastors and pastoral staffs, including musicians, take the time to plan and rehearse every aspect of the worship services, not just the music and sermons. It is likewise true that additional leaders sharing in the design and conducting of worship services means that pastors and other leaders must let go of some responsibility and share it with others—the more the better, at least to some degree. That topic is worth deeper exploration as well.

CHAPTER 10

"Would that all ... were prophets"
Give the Work to the People

As the people of God wandered in the wilderness on their way to the Promised Land, they complained time and again. According to Numbers 11, the complaints of the people that they had no meat to eat initiated a serious conversation between Moses and God. God advised Moses to select elders to share some of the gift of "spirit" God had provided him, and most of the seventy chosen did prophesy—once. Only two elders kept prophesying in the camp, Eldad and Medad. Assuming Moses did not want ongoing competition in leadership, Joshua urged Moses to quiet them. Yet according to scripture, Moses replied that on the contrary he wished everyone possessed God's Spirit and prophesied (Num. 11:29). Instead of trying to keep to himself the gifts for leadership, Moses sought to have the gifts shared even more broadly.

In his classic study of the ministry of Johnny Ray Youngblood at the Saint Paul Community Baptist Church, *Upon This Rock: The Miracle of a Black Church*, Samuel Freedman points to the use of this text by the pastor. Youngblood named a men's group "The Eldads and Medads" and met with them in discussion regularly on Tuesday evenings. Freedman could see in the meetings and the results in ministry how shared leadership helped black men gain voice and confidence, how it brought in new young men to the fellowship, and how the women of the congregation became curious and threatened in jest to start another group—the "Elmom-Memoms."[1]

Story after story about Youngblood indicates his joy in sharing power and leadership. In one particular sequence, two men told him they had received God's call to safeguard vehicles during worship services. Youngblood commissioned them (an act of administration) to a "Ministry of Parking." Again, Freedman tells of Youngblood working with congregational leaders to open schools, transform standard programs for young people into Yoke fellows and cheer-leading teams, offer a day camp, open arts classes, and more.

Research in congregations brings additional insights from pastors, members of staff, and from lay leaders as well. Consider the situation of Larry Chapin, whose congregation provides some good illustrations in every one of the topics already explored.

Larry Chapin

As Larry Chapin and I talked about the Chester Church and his first year as pastor there, a phone call interrupted us.

"Excuse me," he said as he picked up the receiver. "Yes, Jen?"

(Pause while he listened.)

"Yes. I see. I think we can wait. He's out of town until next Tuesday, I think. I'd like him to know everything you and I know before we go ahead, and there's no real crunch. We have the time.

(Pause while he listened.)

"Yes. Good idea. Please do. 'Bye."

"That was our bookkeeper," Larry explained to me. "She is ready to send out several year-end benevolence checks approved by the mission committee. The money is there to cover it, but she is a bit uncomfortable about cash levels going into the New Year because of a bridge loan that the session just authorized for the building program. The committee chair is out of town for a few days, and it's important that he knows exactly where things stand. I don't want him to be surprised, or hindered later. She said she would call him and leave word so he can follow up."

Here was administration as pastoral care—done instinctively and efficiently. I noted his intuitive respect for lay authority, his positive response to a staff member, and his succinct conversation.

Pastor Larry Chapin serves a growing congregation in a town not far from Richmond. Entering ministry after careers in both law and financial services, he left Wall Street to enter seminary. His wife and two sons, another soon to arrive, came too. After seminary, he served a strong, two hundred-year-old church just outside a small but growing Appalachian city. It was there he first began to read about pastors and other church leaders as "entrepreneurs."

> In church circles, this term always had a negative connotation. Now, here it was being spoken of positively, as a way of conceiving how pastors and other church leaders "make things happen." It certainly fit my business experience and affirmed my intuition about how organizations move forward. It was a mindset that I was accustomed to, one that matched up well with my natural inclination to open dealings with others. It gave me a new level of assurance and a sense of greater freedom in my work.
>
> One of the keys is being attentive enough and patient enough to recognize where it is that new energy is already being manifested, where it is that things are already happening. Then it's a matter of encouraging some, and prompting others to move forward, tapping into their own sense of freedom while helping them negotiate their way to the end result we're hoping for.

The Chester Church had almost no full-time staff for a congregation of about a thousand when he arrived a year ago. The youth minister had moved on, as had the Christian educator. Larry worked with the congregation to see the possibility for a new design for staffing, one that would be more integrated and organic. "I explained my vision, and I helped in the process of forming committees, and then trusted them to do the work."

"In leading congregations, there is always a balance between freedom and control. It's risky," he confessed. "Some people thrive, others struggle. Interest in outcome can be misunderstood as manipulation. I try to let folks know what I think while leaving space for alternative wisdom and results that are different from what I have imagined."

> For example, we hired a consultant for our capital campaign. The elder who chaired the search had just gained

experience from a search in another place, so he knew what was involved. Tim is a very deliberate person, however, and a few of us chafed a bit as he methodically went about setting up interviews with several firms. After we met with the second consulting group, there was a strong feeling that we had found the right thing to do. I was going to be out of town on the evening of the final interview, but suggested that they proceed without me. That's what they did.

That night, after the final interview, they took a vote and decided to go with the second group. But some on the committee felt that the proposed fee was a bit high. After a lively discussion, they decided to contact the second group, which then responded with a discount. This all took place before the final meeting, which I was able to attend. That night, the committee decided to move forward, with an even greater hopefulness. There was hard work ahead, but I felt even more assured that we had a good fit.

Letting go seems very difficult for most pastors, educators, and administrators. Honestly, it seems equally difficult initially for lay leaders in congregations. There is within local churches a tendency to defer to decisions made by staff, even to seek staff decisions at every turn. It seems both professional staff and lay leaders must learn and adopt "letting go" as a part of a healthy congregational culture.

Larry Chapin told me that as he now supervises a new associate pastor and a director of learning ministries, he tries to repeat constantly that they, too, have permission to "make things happen." Moreover, he encourages them personally when they do show initiative, and he asks how he can support them. In addition, along with lay leaders in governing body meetings, he calls attention to the work led by each person—professional and lay—in ways that encourage everyone to keep it up. Larry also acknowledges his indebtedness to those who have come before to nurture such a culture. Again, our familiar image of geese flying in formation comes to mind, with the increase in range this method affords the geese, rather than each goose facing wind resistance alone.

When I called attention to Larry's seemingly intuitive response to the bookkeeper, which to my mind had so clearly sought not to undercut the work of the lay leader, he responded: "Yes, that is one transaction. Relationships are built on thousands of transactions. Almost every time, the relationship is going to be more important than the transaction. That's how trust is built and flourishes. People will know that they can expect that from you, and mutual trust and respect will grow."

Larry Chapin is considering the effects of small and huge transactions alike as he shares leadership. He also is conscious of the relationship between letting go and his enhanced capacity for leadership. The one pastoral movement gives away power and control, in many respects, without counting the cost. The opposite movement, simultaneously, draws everyone together toward unity in mission and centered worship and work. This centrifugal letting go mysteriously permits and enhances a centripetal drawing together.

Some years ago, a colleague who helped congregations study their common work and worship described a healthy congregation as one with two strong arms and with a vital heart and circulatory system. One arm stretches out in mission, and the other arm enfolds men and women in evangelism, while the heart and circulatory system feed the whole body in nurture and joyful worship together. This attractive image, with the one arm extended in giving and the other gathering in new participants, helps in imagining what the gift of letting go accomplishes. Larry Chapin seems not only to be cognizant of this counterintuitive truth, but also he seems to be heartened and motivated in ministry by its veracity. At other congregations, it was apparent that pastors and lay leaders did the same. In routine matters, this giving and receiving, going and coming, was highlighted in stories they told. A couple of instances:

Kate McGregor Mosely

One of the resident pastors at Central Presbyterian spoke of both intuiting and also gaining this insight in the course of her work. As one of the members of the Strategic Planning Committee, she chafed at first about the amount of time spent in Bible study, at the slow pace of the committee resolutions of issues, and even resisted the phrase "strategic planning" as unnecessarily corporate. She sought instead to have words like vision and discernment employed—words she considered more appropriate for a church.

As the group met, she sensed also that Pastor Gary Charles was annoyed by the slow pace of the meetings. He had asked them to present a draft of the strategic plan in six months. But after that time they were still writing preambles for each of the sections.

"Both of us had to let go," she reported. "It is not easy to give over control, direction, and timing, and I still think it could have been done more quickly. But I had the sense the results would justify the delay. They did."

"One of the other members had good experience in planning, and she helped us when we came to deciding what goals to include and which to consolidate. She had good experience in seeing what she called 'divergence' and 'convergence.' We moved pretty quickly in the end, and the long work in preparation paid off."

Steve Law

When he began work as the church business administrator at South Highland Church in Birmingham, Alabama, Steve Law was pulled from regular work in early January to consider the plight of a recently employed church custodian, who expressed despair at his financial plight—behind in rent, utility payments, and understandably despondent as a result. Law remembers a church secretary approaching him the same morning, showing him an error in her W-2 tax form and seeking redress.

In giving priority to the more external matter—hours of phone calls and counseling to gather the funds for the custodian—the South Highland Church met the considerable need and drew closer together as a trusting congregation. When Steve told those interested in helping financially that their gifts for an individual would not be tax deductible, they told him they did not care. He said the need of the secretary for proper records and pay was subsequently met as well. And he was soon able to engage in the myriad end-of-year details for regular congregational life and accountability.

What Steve Law, Kate Mosely, and Larry Chapin experienced was some anxiety in letting go, but also exhilaration in having other leaders share the burden and see other gifted people emerge as leaders. Some books analyze this process quite well.

Leadership without Easy Answers

Ronald Heifitz, a psychiatrist on the faculty of the Kennedy School at Harvard, has been for me the most helpful proponent of shared leadership. In order to teach leadership, Heifitz, in *Leadership without Easy Answers*, takes examples from the Bible and other classical texts; from the work of such luminaries as Martin Luther King Jr., Mohandas Gandhi, Margaret Sanger, and William Ruckleshaus; and from cases he disguised to protect privacy. "Give the work back to the people," he urges frequently. It is the responsibility of a leader to "regulate the distress," if possible, but many must be sharing in leadership for healthy, constructive change to occur. In his words, *"Give the work back to the people, but at a rate they can stand."* Place and develop responsibility by putting the pressure on the people with the problem. What Heifitz describes here about modulating the stress in a group is actually and perhaps surprisingly an administrative activity.[2]

Heifitz distinguishes "leading with authority" from "leading without authority." Actually, the more proper division is between "formal" and "informal" power. In our church context, pastors, staff members, and most of the lay leaders in a congregation possess formal authority, vested in them with their selection, call, and in some cases, ordination to office. In every one of these cases, however, the authority is also informal in nature, for the officer with formal authority must remain popular among the members of the congregation in order to accomplish anything, indeed in order even to be heard. And in most church forms of government, the power of the pastor and any pastoral staff, certainly of lay leaders, is heavily circumscribed in formal decision-making.

Obviously, to follow the argument of this book, the administrative work necessary in the function of the office enhances the occasions for informal pastoral care, which in turn increases the leadership capability of the officer. In Heifitz's words, "Formal authorization brings with it the powers of an office, but informal authorization brings the subtle yet substantial power to extend one's reach way beyond the limits of the job description."[3]

So power is gathered both from one's designation to a particular office, but more from gaining "the respect, trust, admiration, and fear of her colleagues." Heifitz also tells of courageous and creative people without authority, in the civil rights struggle, for example, of their work of suasion and example in informal leadership. More profoundly yet, he points time and again to the reciprocal nature of leadership and authority—how sharing leadership when one exercises formal authority leads to increased effectiveness, and how sharing effective informal authority may prove the more powerful yet.[4]

Specifically, in response to the temptation named earlier in this study as "Distance Dissent," Heifitz advises those with authority: "Give cover to those who raise hard questions and generate distress—people who point to the internal contradictions of the society [congregation]. These individuals often will have latitude to provoke rethinking that authorities do not have."[5]

Excellent explorations of other of Heifitz's insights in church settings include those by Anthony Robinson, especially his *Transforming Congregational Culture*.[6]

They also warn, as does Heifitz himself, that congregational leadership can be frustrating and even perilous. Suffice it here to point briefly to other pertinent areas in which Heifitz' work can enhance understanding of church administration as pastoral care.

Heifitz observes that leadership is "both active and reflexive. One has to alternate between participating and observing." In an extended metaphor, he suggests that leaders need both to be in the dance and to see the dance from the balcony. "Getting on the balcony" is his expression for discerning significant issues and directing attention appropriately toward addressing them.

To lead in congregations is both to mix it up in the work and worship underway, but also to discern the real issues and to marshal the resources toward meeting those issues. The work of church administration, honestly, can be directed toward the cure of souls if pastors, staff, and lay leaders are all able to "get on the balcony" as well as "dance in the dance." So those invited into positions of responsibility, invitations to give and to join in work, training and education, devotional and worship time, assessment and follow through are all focused on the mission of the congregation.[7]

A second insight proves equally important. Heifitz argues for developing partners to accomplish the work. He distinguishes two kinds of partners—confidants and allies. The confidant has permission to give correction and critique without fear and is even encouraged to "be the devil's advocate" in order to achieve good decisions. The confidant is a friend. The ally may well be in opposition, may even be an enemy, but is encouraged as well to share in leadership and receives some of the rewards of success. The ally can have common interest even with different and sometimes contrary goals. Heifitz says clearly that "an authority should protect those whom he wants to silence."[8]

Honestly, it seems that letting go to lead is both the most difficult and the most effective practice for leaders of congregations. It applies to committee chairs, youth directors, musicians, and pastors alike. It requires developing a perspective that values partners, whether they are confidants or allies, voices echoing the same chorus or those offering some measure of dissonance. And it involves supporting those to whom tasks and decisions have been entrusted—supporting them even when the outcome is not precisely what the one in formal authority had envisaged.

Developing perspective to direct congregational administration toward deepening pastoral care and the nurture of believers might take repentance, and it certainly takes practice. Some, such as Gary Charles or Fairfax Fair, might act intuitively. But, as Ed Stock and Larry Chapin stated they learned to do, they probably developed the ability to let others lead and support them. Yet the perspective involves more than just this ability. It requires practices of leadership with several dimensions, or elements—practices and issues to be considered in the concluding chapter that follows.

CHAPTER 11

"Grace and peace to you…"
A Concluding Letter to
Congregational Leaders

Dear Colleagues in Ministry,

By the grace of God, you and I are entrusted with responsibility for a portion of the people of God. We are called and charged to help lead congregations of Christians.

We administer these congregations as a way of caring for those who belong to them. In turn, those believers and we join to care for many others. Because we are human, our questions about ministry may frequently be little ones: How can we avoid trivia? How can we do a job more quickly? How can we put up with another meeting?

I hope that we can constantly ask bigger, more mature questions: How can we administer congregations in ways most likely to increase the measure of pastoral care? How can our service, in menial and glorious work alike, build up the body of Christ? How can all the work and worship in this congregation help God's work of redemption and release in the world?

In asking the big questions and in practicing church administration as pastoral care—placing the scutwork in proper perspective—we help our congregations thrive.

And personally, I can testify that gaining perspective helps much more than following any list of particulars in church leadership. Thinking of the administrative work using various management "tools" from a pastoral "toolbox" proved unhelpful, sometimes leading to manipulative behavior on my part. Working from a pastoral perspective and organic images of leadership, especially biblical ones, has made the most sense and proven the most enduring help.

Through the congregations studied, and through research on the subject over several years, I find certain important elements in this perspective, several dimensions to the project to redeem pastoral scutwork. These dimensions I do not think of as "rules" or "keys" so much as considerations and practices.

Each of these dimensions may not be of equal use to everyone. Each congregation calls for distinct leadership and management, and every leader possesses a distinctive style. Even the perspective might well be altered by the circumstances of a particular church. As the congregational studies Gang of Five warned, there is no recipe for salvation, no formula for guaranteed success.

Here, with the disclaimer of no "silver bullets," are seven of the most important things we can do to ensure that administration serves as pastoral care:

1. Steward God's Grace
2. Build Teams
3. Welcome Constructive Change
4. Seek to Grow Personally
5. Remain Modest
6. Cultivate Intuition
7. Exercise Imagination

1. Steward God's Grace

To engage in administration from a pastoral care point of view is first to remember that we are called to be "good stewards of the manifold grace of God," as 1 Peter urges, so that we can "serve one another with whatever gift each of you has received" (4:10). Paul says he considers himself, and others bearing witness, as "stewards of God's mysteries" (1 Cor. 4:1). The leaders in congregations that "have it all together," folk such as those at White Memorial, Trinity, and the rest, seem to treat administration as stewardship. They surely think of themselves as stewards—the pastors, the staff, and the lay leaders together. They "pay the rent," and they go miles beyond that necessity.

They carefully design the best ways to respond gratefully to the gifts provided for that congregation's life.

Interestingly, as I spoke with lay leaders, church administrators, educators, and pastors, many of them spoke frequently of gifts and grace. Dick Keever, in reading the chapter in this book about organization of finances, in which his charge Bayside Presbyterian was featured, said that Paul's treatment of gifts, grace, and giving in 2 Corinthians receives too little attention. "It is the center of our whole program and of our planning," he said. "It is impossible to emphasize gifts, grace, and giving too much in a local church." He told of first arriving and of preaching and teaching about stewardship of time, money, and gifts. One member complained that he focused too much on this, while others said, "Keep it up!" Then she too "came around," in Dick's words, and became more deeply involved in the church and in its mission.

Certainly the helpful perspective for congregational leaders includes considering everyone as stewards, not owners of the church. Indeed, 1 Peter cautions stewards not to "lord it over" one another (5:3). An effective perspective also includes thinking in terms of teamwork, not "stardom." It is fair to speak of the work in the perfect tense: they "have built" teams. But they care more about the ongoing process, and therefore the active present is more appropriate as they see the challenge: "they build teams."

2. Build Teams

In every congregation I interviewed, the leaders kept speaking of others who should be included in my profile. At Third Presbyterian, Richmond, people spoke repeatedly of the desire of Pastor Steve Hartman to include as many as possible in the leadership of the church. "The Bible speaks of the communion of saints," Nelson Ould explained. "That's the permission Steve Hartman provides—for tasks to be shared and for us to provide insight and prayer for one another." At White Memorial the pastoral staff and the support staff alike told of people pitching in and of the need to find even more folks to move into positions of responsibility. At Highland Presbyterian, pastors and lay leaders alike refer to the multiple efforts for visitation. Many teams work together to make certain those in particular need of care receive lots of it, and everyone receives at least some.

The team perspective, it seems, trumps clericalism in the congregations studied—strong as that force might be today. Pastors found various ways of emphasizing collegial responsibility among lay leaders and pastoral staffs. At Highland, lay leaders tell the pastors whom to see, and the whole visiting effort is supervised by the session. At Third, lay leaders take part in seasonal worship planning, and staff members give one another ideas and examples for upcoming sermons.

Leaders in the congregations spoke of the organizational problems that arose when someone—lay or clergy—operates with a "silo mentality" (a phrase many used negatively). Tom Faracco said that was the style he had encountered elsewhere, and he rejoiced that Pine Street Church seemed to have none of it.

3. Welcome Constructive Change

Change is a reality in the lives of everyone. The pace of change is increasing, as most of these congregational profiles indicate. Many of the changes occur beyond the control of congregational leaders. White Memorial faced a retirement; Purity Presbyterian in South Carolina faced a succession of church secretaries in a single year. Several of the churches expected officers taking responsibility in new "classes" or the completion of terms of service. These changes one might call "anticipated personnel changes."

Other personnel changes are unexpected. Already in the months since the beginning of this research project, other changes in personnel, some unforeseen during the interviews, have taken place. Nelson Ould and Steve Hartman assumed additional responsibilities with the purchase of property that might become a second site for Third. Dick Keever has accepted a call to become chaplain at a nearby retirement home. Kristy Hubert, who coordinated visiting at Highland, received "an offer she could not turn down" from a network of rehabilitation centers.

But the changes most interesting to observe, and most important in considering pastoral perspective, are the complex cultural changes chosen to allow more effective work and worship—moving toward a team approach to administration, for example, and changes in ways of governing and stewardship.

Some of the change results from choices, such as the way governance takes place at Central or the way worship changes at Third. Part of the organization for change is permitting a congregation, in the words of Carl Dudley, to "move beyond 'familiarity blindness' to rediscover their turf."[1] Dudley was speaking of organization for social ministry, but his advice applies across the board.

Most of those interviewed spoke fondly of the willingness of people to change—changing ways of holding meetings, including a form of testimony in worship, developing new ministries at Trinity. All these grew from conscious decisions by lay leaders, staff, and pastors. It's the way Roy Terry describes the summoning of gifts for contemporary worship services at the church he serves: "What was so magnificent about this experience was that all these gifts arose out of the congregation. Nothing was forced. Rather, through worship people connected in new ways and found a desire to share what they had to offer."[2]

4. Seek to Grow Personally

Those interviewed kept asking as well as telling. As they told of the work of the congregations they served, lay leaders, pastors, musicians, Christian educators, and administrators all asked persistently about what could be learned from others. Interviews became conversations about best practices, Bible, and theology. As they received these book chapters in draft to check for accuracy and improvement, most of those interviewed commented on pregnant possibilities in the other congregations I had studied.

Gradually, I began to ask more questions about the habits of congregational leaders in reading, engaging in continuing education, and comparing practices with others elsewhere in similar positions of responsibility. Everyone I questioned said they took the study time and the vacation time afforded in their calls and contracts. Lay leaders spoke of wanting more instruction in their particular areas of the work. In fact, at Sunburst the high-class volunteer program that captivated the imaginations of congregants was built on the twin pillars of regular supervision and funds for study elsewhere.

5. Remain Modest

If those interviewed sought further education and honing of skills, it was equally true that they generally remained modest about their own parts in the effective work examined and their parts in building healthy congregational cultures. Several actually questioned whether their congregation should be studied. "Others are probably doing lots better than we are" was a common refrain.

Modesty is equated by some with low self-esteem, but it seems to me that it comes from competence, confidence, and healthy respect of others. Of course, the fact that New Testament writers caution believers to remain modest should be authority enough for everyone to pursue it (Luke 18:9–14; Rom. 12:3).

One could argue that mainline Christians in general maintain modesty in their assertion of religious beliefs. This blessing and curse, two sides of the same truth, both frustrate those who would have absolute certainty and draw those who deeply respect opposing points of view. Leaders of congregations especially might be tempted to declarations that are self-righteous and exclusive. But studies of institutions over time show those of hottest fire, where doubts and debate have no space, are of shorter duration than those that offer more room for tolerance and growth.

6. Cultivate Intuition

Leaders spoke of coming to trust their own intuitions about matters of administration and pastoral care. Ed Stock and Fairfax Fair both told of coming to trust increasingly their intuitive powers and insight. The same development can be observed in the narratives of Gary Charles, Steve Hartman, Debbie McKinley, and others. They had immediate perceptions of needed changes, and they persisted in advocating for them.

This phenomenon of intuition—immediate perception—has been explored by Malcolm Gladwell, albeit for the general public and not just for leaders of Christian congregations. In his surprise best-seller *Blink*, Gladwell contended that "decisions made very quickly can be every bit as good as decisions made cautiously and deliberately." Likewise, he argued that sometimes intuition can be misguided. Third, and most important, he found that intuition can be cultivated in a disciplined way, so that over time it can become more reliable. Human judgment becomes more accurate with experience. In the words of Gladwell, "snap judgments and first impressions can be educated and controlled."[3]

Gladwell's argument applies in congregational contexts as well. Thus Don Simpson knew to ask those who were critical to help him. Thus Ed Stock explained that his hunches in each succeeding church throughout his ministry became more dependable. He could move in Second Presbyterian, Lexington, Kentucky, to try asking for information about individuals' giving that he had not previously requested—information that proved valuable—without disrupting the culture; this led to better stewardship in the congregation. Thus Kate Mosely, apprentice in the work, already could exercise strong leadership in hosting a conference. Thus Gary Charles knew intuitively as he came to Central that the governing body was too large, ineffective, and could be divided in two parts. And thus Larry Chapin could instinctively rely upon lay leadership in a "transaction" on the phone, in order to build capacity for leadership in the Chester church. All of them trusted and relied on rapid human judgment.

In congregational life, too frequently leaders rely on outside resources or on mechanical indicators for decision-making. They are not willing to rely on their own collective wisdom or individual discernment for administrative solutions and directions. Among these who exhibit best practices in congregational leadership, however, boldness and courage show the other side of modesty and reliance on a team. Like the orchestra conductor who prepares and then rehearses to perform the music, the congregational leader and the team together keep developing the practice of excellent preparation, execution, and assessment to improve yet more. Such discipline and developed intuition is not conjured. Christians believe it is a gift from God.

7. Exercise Imagination

In the course of studying congregations, time and again I admired the creative ways leaders found of handling particular organizational and administrative situations. The naming of administrator Billy Ricketts to be Director of Congregational Ministries at Second Presbyterian, Norfolk, Virginia, placed administration and authority in outreach in capable hands. The accountability of committees to the "Ministries" at Central, Atlanta, kept authority and responsibility clear but also permitted members and officers at every level of church life to share in both. Deacons providing pastoral prayers at Old Pine in Philadelphia, worship services staggered five minutes at Third, Richmond—on and on go the examples of creative organizational patterns and administrative innovation, all opening possibilities for better, deeper, and wider pastoral care.

The recognition of Mary Henry at Highland as leader represents a special kind of creativity. By the pastoral staff and lay leaders alike, she is honored as a part of the team, though she dissents from the "business-like" emphasis on numbers and organization. In that church she is a kind of "counter-conductor," like the French horn player who kept the beat while the orchestra conductor sought to evoke emotions with her sweeping gestures and swaying body. The formal leaders at Highland are attending to the inclusion of dissenters, the point Heifitz values. All of these and more illustrate the creativity of people and communities.

A few years ago, Craig Dykstra, a theologian and Senior Vice President for Religion at the Lilly Endowment, began exploring "pastoral imagination" as a phrase to describe the special perspective cultivated by effective ministers.[4] The phrase does well in describing not just the creative work of formally ordained clergy, but indeed of every congregational leader. Drawing on Howard Gardner, who developed a theory of multiple intelligences, Dykstra claimed that scripture; discernment of the gospel demands; preaching, teaching, and leading worship; exercising discipline in responding to human need; and administering a congregation all combine over time to infuse a distinctive intelligence that is crucial for effective ministry. Craig's explorations struck a chord of deep truth among many pastors and others in church leadership. Now the term is employed widely, and it helps declare the nature of the perspective.

In one sense, the experiences of the congregational leader are provided by others. They come as gifts. Personally, I remember going straight from seminary to be a supply pastor for several years at a congregation in rural North Carolina, one described as "cantankerous" by the presbytery executive.

I found the church of farming families my best theological professor; and I think they enjoyed their role in educating the naïf. When the farmers experienced a drought the second summer, one of them asked me to "Pray rain." In my best seminary graduate fashion I began to explain the vast providence of God, how rain in one area meant drought in another. He interrupted me and declared, "Son. Preacher can't pray rain ain't worth nothin'.'" This curmudgeonly old farmer contributed mightily to my wisdom thereafter on the expectations of prayers being answered, an expectation that has deepened my prayer and my sense of the organization of a congregation (or a seminary) to depend on the practice of prayer.

James Glasse spoke of "paying the rent" in order freely to exercise ministry as one sees it. If I have paid the rent in this effort, then permit me to close the book and this open letter with a brief homily on 1 Peter 5. I take the lexicon of development officers, who made the noun "gift" into a verb.

Receive Administration as God Gifts It

"I exhort the elders among you to tend the flock of God that is in your charge, exercising the oversight not under compulsion but willingly, as God would have you do it—not for sordid gain but eagerly. Do not lord it over those in your charge, but be examples to your flock" (1 Peter 5:1b–3).

The closing chapter (chapter 5) of this pastoral letter of encouragement comes to believers with some advice for "leaders among you" (more literally, "fellow elders"). It was evidently written to churches in Asia Minor at a time when threats of persecution loomed, or at least when Christians needed extra discipline in the face of adversity.[5]

My closing chapter also emphasizes the care of souls as a pastoral perspective for congregational leaders, "fellow elders," engaged in administration. The perspective is one for all those in congregational leadership, not just those named "pastors." But I have yet to see a congregation in which an effective team does not include the pastor, or the whole pastoral staff in larger churches for that matter.

Succinctly put, 1 Peter describes the perspective found in excellent congregational leaders—pastors, members of pastoral staffs, educators, musicians, business administrators, lay leaders, and all the rest. The concluding passage in 1 Peter contains three pieces of advice offered together as contrasting goals: Do not compel or feel compelled, but act freely and willingly as God intends. Do not seek your own gain, but be eager in service. And do not "lord it over those in your charge," but be examples to those for whom you have responsibility. That New Testament letter also warns about temptations and exhorts leaders to humble themselves, to keep alert, and to anticipate redemption. First Peter says, "And after you have suffered for a little while, the God of all grace, who has called you to his eternal glory in Christ, will himself restore, support, strengthen, and establish you" (5:10).

Doing church scutwork, the menial work especially, is scarcely what 1 Peter would consider suffering. But I am sure that at times it seems tedious and trivial to all of us. Seeing church administration as pastoral care, and engaging it effectively to open and deepen pastoral relations, is a gift given by the God of all charisms. Having oversight in a congregation today may not be much different from the work of the early elders. But such stewardship of a Christian community is not easy. Encouragement from the Bible, from the wisdom of those who followed Jesus and were first to organize Christian congregations, may be enough to keep us pressing on. But I imagine the work and examples from those among us doing superb work in leading congregational life can also be models for us.

Grace and Peace to You

The closing words of 1 Peter, "Peace to all of you who are in Christ" (5:14b), echo the openings and closings of most of the New Testament letters. Early leaders were forever wishing grace or peace or both to one another in the name of Jesus Christ. It is an appropriate conclusion for a study concerned with administration and pastoral care.

How can we administer congregations in ways most likely to increase the measure of pastoral care? We see examples of small and large congregations accomplishing the work well, and leaders speak of God's gifts, the work of many leaders gracefully collaborating.

How can our service, in menial and glorious work alike, build up the body of Christ? That, too, is the working of God's grace finally. The Holy Spirit quickens faith and gives direction to the church.

How can all the work and worship in this congregation help God's work of redemption and release in the world? Each of us asks that question as a prayer, more than as a practical problem to be solved. We may lament, in words attributed to French Catholic Alfred Loisy, "Lord, you promised us the kingdom, but all we got was the church!" But God's word responds, "My grace is sufficient" (2 Cor. 12:9). We draw joy in ministry, satisfaction in leadership, fulfillment in service, and faith from the examples of other faithful—all divine gifts. And mysteriously, others are drawn into the company of the redeemed—the joyful, the miraculously fulfilled.

And Christians receive God's loving peace, or at least a partial and promising glimpse of it, from time to time in worship and work. Now we know it only in part; then we will know it, even as we have been fully known (cf. 1 Cor. 13:12).

Following Ephesians: "Peace be to the community, and love with faith, from God the Father and the Lord Jesus Christ. Grace be with all who have an undying love of our Lord Jesus Christ" (6:23–24). Amen.

NOTES

CHAPTER 1, CHURCH ADMINISTRATION AND PASTORAL CARE

1. Pierre Sauvage, *Les Armes de l'Esprit* (1989), produced by Friends of Le Chambon, FR3 Films Productions.
2. William V. Arnold, *Introduction to Pastoral Care* (Philadelphia: Westminster, 1982), 39.
3. Browne Barr, *High-Flying Geese: Unexpected Reflections on the Church and Its Ministry* (Minneapolis: Seabury, 1983).

CHAPTER 2, THE MINISTERIAL SURPRISE OF SCUTWORK

1. James D. Glasse, *Putting It Together in the Parish* (Nashville: Abingdon, 1972), 56.
2. Robert N. Bacher and Michael Cooper-White, *Church Administration: Programs, Process, Purpose* (Minneapolis: Fortress, 2007), vii.
3. Mike Bonem and Roger Patterson, *Leading from the Second Chair: Serving Your Church, Fulfilling Your Role, and Realizing Your Dreams* (San Francisco: Jossey-Bass, 2005).
4. Jackson Carroll, Carl Dudley, and William McKinney, eds., *Handbook for Congregational Studies* (Nashville: Abingdon, 1986), 81.
5. Jackson W. Carroll, *God's Potters: Pastoral Leadership and the Shaping of Congregations* (Grand Rapids: Eerdmans, 2006), 103ff.
6. Ibid., 109, 115.

7. Mark D. Constantine, *Travelers on the Journey: Pastors Talk of Their Lives and Commitments* (Grand Rapids: Eerdmans, 2005), 209, 212.

CHAPTER 3, HAS THERE ALWAYS BEEN SCUTWORK?

1. General indebtedness to John T. McNeill, *History of the Cure of Souls* (New York: Harper, 1951).
2. Douglas Schuurman, *Vocations: Discerning Our Calling in Life* (Grand Rapids: Eerdmans, 2004), 37.
3. John Calvin, Geneva Ordnances, *Opera quae supersunt omnia*, translated in Fred Graham, *The Constructive Revolutionary: John Calvin and his Socio-Economic Impact* (Richmond: John Knox, 1971), 99.
4. Ibid., 113.
5. On the origins of the Puritan revolution, which he terms "a culture of discipline," see William Hunt, *The Puritan Movement: The Coming Revolution in an English Colony* (Cambridge: Harvard, 1983). See also James F. Cooper, *Tenacious of Their Liberties: The Congregationalists of Colonial Massachusetts* (New York: Oxford, 1999), on shared leadership in administration and pastoral care in a colony.
6. Louis Weeks, "The Incorporation of American Religion: The Case of the Presbyterians," *Religion and American Culture* 1, no. 1 (Winter 1991): 101–118, revised subsequently in Milton J Coalter, John M. Mulder, and Louis B. Weeks, eds., *The Organizational Revolution: Presbyterians and American Denominationalism* (Louisville: Westminster/John Knox, 1992).
7. Debby Applegate, *The Most Famous Man in America: The Biography of Henry Ward Beecher* (New York: Three Leaves Press, 2006), 145, 146.
8. Brooks Holifield, *God's Ambassadors: A History of Christian Clergy in America* (Grand Rapids: Eerdmans, 2007), 159ff, quoting G. B. Willcox, *The Pastor Amidst His Flock* (New York: American Tract Society, 1890).
9. Ibid., 160.
10. H. Richard Niebuhr, *The Purpose of the Church and Its Ministry* (New York: Harper, 1956), 1–49.

11. Holifield, 246–251.
12. Thomas C. Campbell and Gary B. Reierson, *The Gift of Administration: Theological Bases for Ministry* (Philadelphia: Westminster, 1981), 37. General indebtedness, as well, to this provocative book.

CHAPTER 4, TWO EFFECTIVE CONGREGATIONS

1. Ann R. Held, *Keeping Faith in Families: A Guide to Worship and Witness in the Home* (Belleville, IL: Mariners, 1987); *Nurturing the Seeds of Spirituality: Families and Congregations Working Together* (Arvada, CO: Mariners, 1998).
2. James Hopewell, *Congregation: Stories and Structures* (Philadelphia: Fortress, 1987), 5.

CHAPTER 5, TEMPTATIONS IN MINISTRY

1. Frances Taylor Gench, "Arguing About Scripture: Johannine Epistles, Presbyterians, and Dirty Laundry (1 John 2:18–25 and 4; 2 John; Psalm 51)," inaugural address, Union Theological Seminary and Presbyterian School of Christian Education, Richmond, Virginia, May 4, 2007.
2. David Canada, *Spiritual Leadership in the Small Member Church* (Nashville: Abingdon, 2005), 16.
3. T. S. Eliot, "The Love Song of J. Alfred Prufrock," *Prufrock, and other Observations* (London: The Egoist, Ltd., 1917).
4. Thomas Hoyt Jr., "Testimony," in Dorothy Bass, ed., *Practicing Our Faith: A Way of Life for a Searching People* (San Francisco: Jossey-Bass, 1997), 92.
5. N. Graham Standish, *Becoming a Blessed Church: Forming a Church of Spiritual Purpose, Presence, and Power* (Herndon, VA: Alban Institute, 2005), 7. See chapter 2, passim.
6. Mihály Csikszentmihályi, *Flow: The Psychology of Optimal Experience* (New York: Harper Perennial, 1990).
7. Thomas W. Currie III, *The Joy of Ministry* (Louisville: Westminster/John Knox, 2008), 4, 5.
8. Ibid., 111.

CHAPTER 6, GOVERNANCE THAT GROWS LEADERS

1. John Robert Smith, *The Church That Stayed: The Life and Times of Central Presbyterian Church in the Heart of Atlanta, 1858–1978* (Atlanta: Historical Society, 1979).
2. Steven Eason, *Making Disciples, Making Leaders: A Manual for Developing Church Officers* (Louisville: Geneva Press, 2004), 66, 67.
3. Ibid., 85.

CHAPTER 7, ORGANIZING MINISTRIES FOR VISITING

1. Linda Raymond and Bill Ellison, *Like Jacob's Well: The Very Human History of Highland Presbyterian Church* (Louisville: Beechmont Press, 2008), 5, 6.
2. Ibid., 178, 179.
3. See www.hpc-lou.org, especially "Member Care."
4. Browne Barr, *The Well-Church Book* (New York: Seabury, 1976), 99.
5. Brooks Holifield, *God's Ambassadors: A History of Christian Clergy in America* (Grand Rapids: Eerdmans, 2007), 161–163.
6. Kennon Callahan, *Twelve Keys to an Effective Church* (New York: Harper & Row, 1997), passim.
7. Ibid., 11.

CHAPTER 8, STEWARDSHIP AND MINISTRY

1. Brian Kluth, http://kluth.org, especially http://kluth.org/WhatShouldPastorsKnowAboutGiving.htm. This website offers significant resources for teaching stewardship.
2. Thomas Jeavons and Rebekah Basinger, *Growing Givers' Hearts: Treating Fundraising as Ministry* (San Francisco: Jossey-Bass, 2000).

CHAPTER 9, ADMINISTRATION FOR WORSHIP

1. General indebtedness to Hughes Oliphant Gibbons, *A History of Old Pine Street* (Philadelphia: Winston, 1905), esp. 17–233.

CHAPTER 10, GIVE THE WORK TO THE PEOPLE

1. Samuel G. Freedman, *Upon This Rock: The Miracles of a Black Church* (New York: HarperCollins, 1993), 58–60.
2. Ronald A. Heifitz, *Leadership without Easy* Answers (Cambridge: Harvard/Belknap, 1994). General indebtedness, esp. 125–148, 252, 262, 263.
3. Ibid., 102.
4. Ibid., 101, 225–240.
5. Ibid., 128.
6. Anthony B. Robinson, *Transforming Congregational Culture* (Grand Rapids: Eerdmans, 2005).
7. Heifitz, *Leadership,* 271.
8. Ibid., 101.

CHAPTER 11, A CONCLUDING LETTER

1. Carl Dudley, *Community Ministries: New Challenges, Proven Steps to Faith-Based Initiatives* (Bethesda: Alban Institute, 2002), 107.
2. Roy Terry, "Becoming God's Church," ed. Diana Butler Bass and Joseph Stewart-Sicking, *From Nomads to Pilgrims: Stories from Practicing Congregations* (Herndon, VA: Alban Institute, 2006), 12.
3. Malcolm Gladwell, *Blink: The Power of Thinking without Thinking* (New York: Little, Brown, 2005), 14, 15, and 245–254, "Listening with your eyes."
4. Craig Dykstra, "The Pastoral Imagination," *Initiatives in Religion* (Spring 2001).
5. Paul J. Achtemeier, *A Commentary on 1 Peter.* Hermeneia Ser. (Minneapolis: Augsburg Fortress, 1996), 323.

BIBLIOGRAPHY

Achtemeier, Paul J. *A Commentary on I Peter.* Hermeneia Series. Minneapolis: Augsburg Fortress, 1996.

Ammerman, Nancy, Jackson Carroll, Carl Dudley, and William McKinney. *Studying Congregations: A New Handbook.* Nashville: Abingdon, 1998.

Applegate, Debby. *The Most Famous Man in America: The Biography of Henry Ward Beecher.* New York: Three Leaves Press, 2006.

Arnold, William V. *Introduction to Pastoral Care.* Philadelphia: Westminster, 1982.

Bacher, Robert N., and Michael Cooper-White. *Church Administration: Programs, Process, Purpose.* Minneapolis: Fortress, 2007.

Barna, George. *Today's Pastors.* Ventura: Regal, 1993.

Barr, Browne. *High Flying Geese: Unexpected Reflections on the Church and Its Ministry.* Minneapolis: Seabury, 1983.

———. *Parish Back Talk.* New York: Abingdon, 1964.

———. *The Well Church Book.* New York: Seabury, 1976.

Butler Bass, Diana. *Christianity for the Rest of Us: How the Neighborhood Church Is Transforming the Faith.* San Francisco: HarperSanFrancisco, 2006.

Butler Bass, Diana, and Joseph Stewart-Sicking. *From Nomads to Pilgrims: Stories from Practicing Congregations.* Herndon, VA: Alban Institute, 2006.

Dorothy Bass, ed. *Practicing Our Faith: A Way of Life for a Searching People.* San Francisco: Jossey-Bass, 1997.

Bonem, Mike, and Roger Patterson. *Leading from the Second Chair: Serving Your Church, Fulfilling Your Role, and Realizing Your Dreams.* San Francisco: Jossey-Bass, 2005.

Callahan, Kennon. *Twelve Keys to an Effective Church.* New York: Harper and Row, 1997.

Canada, David. *Spiritual Leadership in the Small Member Church.* Nashville: Abingdon, 2005.

Carroll, Jackson W. *God's Potters: Pastoral Leadership and the Shaping of Congregations.* Grand Rapids: Eerdmans, 2006.

Carroll, Jackson W., Carl Dudley, and William McKinney, eds. *Handbook for Congregational Studies.* Nashville: Abingdon, 1986.

Constantine, Mark D. *Travelers on the Journey: Pastors Talk About Their Lives and Commitments.* Grand Rapids: Eerdmans, 2005.

Cooper, James F. *Tenacious of Their Liberties: The Congregationalists of Colonial Massachusetts.* New York: Oxford, 1999.

Crumroy, Otto F. , Stan Kukawka, and Frank M. Witman, eds. *Church Administration and Finance Manual.* Harrisburg, PA: Morehouse, 1998.

Csikszentmihályi, Mihály. *Flow: The Psychology of Optimal Experience.* New York: Harper Perennial, 1990.

Currie III, Thomas W. *The Joy of Ministry.* Louisville: Westminster/ John Knox, 2008.

Daniel, Lillian. *Tell It Like It Is: Reclaiming the Practice of Testimony.* Herndon, VA: Alban Institute, 2006.

Dittes, James E. *Minister on the Spot.* Philadelphia: Pilgrim, 1970.

Dudley, Carl. *Community Ministries: New Challenges, Proven Steps to Faith-Based Initiatives.* Bethesda: Alban Institute, 2002.

Dykstra, Craig. "The Pastoral Imagination," *Initiatives in Religion,* Occasional Papers from the Lilly Endowment (Spring 2001).

———. *Growing in the Life of Faith: Education and Christian Practices.* 2nd ed. Louisville: Westminster/John Knox, 2005.

Eason, Steven. *Making Disciples, Making Leaders: A Manual for Developing Church Officers.* Louisville: Geneva Press, 2004.

Farley, Edward. *Practicing Gospel: Unconventional Thoughts on the Church's Ministry.* Louisville: Westminster, 2003.

Freedman, Samuel G. *Upon This Rock: The Miracles of a Black Church.* New York: HarperCollins, 1993.

Gench, Frances Taylor. "Arguing About Scripture: Johannine Epistles, Presbyterians, and Dirty Laundry (1 John 2:18–25 and 4; 2 John; Psalm 51)." Inaugural Address, Union Theological Seminary and Presbyterian School of Christian Education, Richmond, Virginia (May 4, 2007).

Gibbons, Hughes Oliphant. *A History of Old Pine Street.* Philadelphia: Winston, 1905.

Glasse, James D. *Profession: Minister.* Nashville: Abingdon, 1968.

Gladwell, Malcolm. *Blink: The Power of Thinking without Thinking.* New York: Little, Brown, 2005.

———. *Putting it Together in the Parish.* Nashville: Abingdon, 1972.

Graham, Fred. *The Constructive Revolutionary: John Calvin and His Socio-Economic Impact.* Richmond: John Knox, 1971

Heifitz, Ronald. *Leadership without Easy Answers.* Cambridge: Harvard/Belknap, 1994.

Held, Ann R. *Keeping Faith in Families: A Guide to Worship and Witness in the Home.* Belleville, IL: Mariners, 1987.

———. *Nurturing the Seeds of Spirituality: Families and Congregations Working Together.* Arvada, CO: Mariners, 1998.

Holifield, Brooks. *God's Ambassadors: A History of Christian Clergy in America.* Grand Rapids: Eerdmans, 2007.

Holmes, Urban. *The Future Shape of the Ministry: A Theological Projection.* New York: Seabury, 1971.

Hopewell, James. *Congregation: Stories and Structures.* Philadelphia: Fortress, 1987.

Hunt, William. *The Puritan Movement: The Coming Revolution in an English Colony.* Cambridge: Harvard, 1983.

Jeavons, Thomas, and Rebekah Basinger. *Growing Givers' Hearts: Treating Fundraising as Ministry.* San Francisco: Jossey-Bass, 2000.

McNeill, John T. *A History of the Cure of Souls.* New York: Harper, 1951.

Powers, Bruce, ed. *Church Administration Handbook.* Nashville: Broadman and Holman,1996.

Raymond, Linda, and William Ellison. *Like Jacob's Well: The Very Human History of Highland Presbyterian Church.* Louisville: Beechmont Press, 2008.

Richardson, Ronald. *Creating a Healthier Church.* Minneapolis: Augsburg, 1996.

Robinson, Anthony. B *Transforming Congregational Culture*. Grand
    Rapids: Eerdmans, 2005.

Schuurman, Douglas. *Vocations: Discerning Our Calling in Life*. Grand
    Rapids: Eerdmans, 2004.

Shawchuck, Norman, and Roger Heuser. *Managing the Congregation*.
    Nashville: Abingdon, 1996.

Smith, John Robert. *The Church That Stayed: The Life and Times of
    Central Presbyterian Church in the Heart of Atlanta, 1858–1978*.
    Atlanta: Atlanta Historical Society, 1979.

Standish, N. Graham. *Becoming a Blessed Church: Forming a Church of
    Spiritual Purpose, Presence, and Power*. Herndon, VA: Alban Institute,
    2005.

Terry, Roy. "Becoming God's Church." In *From Nomads to Pilgrims:
    Stories from Practicing Congregations*, edited by Diana Butler
    Bass and Joseph Stewart-Sicking, 7–16. Herndon, VA: Alban
    Institute, 2006.

Weeks, Louis. "The Incorporation of American Religion: The
    Case of the Presbyterians," in *Religion and American Culture*
    1, no. 1 (Winter 1991): 101–118, revised subsequently in
    Milton J. Coalter, John M. Mulder, and Louis B. Weeks,
    eds., *The Organizational Revolution: Presbyterians and American
    Denominationalism*. Louisville: Westminster/John Knox, 1992.

Welch, Robert H. *Church Administration*. Nashville: Broadman and
    Holman, 2005.

Wind, James P. and James W. Lewis, *American Congregations*. 2 vols.
    Chicago: University of Chicago, 1994.